Palgrave Studies in Economic History

Series Editor
Kent Deng
London School of Economics
London, UK

Palgrave Studies in Economic History is designed to illuminate and enrich our understanding of economies and economic phenomena of the past. The series covers a vast range of topics including financial history, labour history, development economics, commercialisation, urbanisation, industrialisation, modernisation, globalisation, and changes in world economic orders.

Jane Du

Farmland, Farming and Food in the National Economy of China, 1947–2020

A Framework for Understanding China's Agricultural Track Record and Food Security

palgrave
macmillan

Jane Du
The China Institute
SOAS, University of London
London, UK

ISSN 2662-6497 ISSN 2662-6500 (electronic)
Palgrave Studies in Economic History
ISBN 978-3-031-70026-2 ISBN 978-3-031-70027-9 (eBook)
https://doi.org/10.1007/978-3-031-70027-9

This Palgrave Macmillan imprint is published by the registered company Springer Nature Switzerland AG.
The registered company address is: Gewerbestrasse 11, 6330 Cham, Switzerland

Contents

About the Author

Jane Du is a research associate in the China Institute, School of Oriental and African Studies, University of London. An agricultural economist, Du has specialised on the political economy of Chinese agriculture, and the industry-agriculture sectoral relations and their evolution. Her publications on Chinese agriculture have ranged from Mao's collectivisation to Deng's agricultural reform, and the role of agriculture in China's return to the market. Another focus of her research has been on the economic history of China's agricultural growth in conjunction with the industrial era.

List of Figures

List of Tables

CHAPTER 1

Food Sector in Chinese Industrialisation Under Mao

Abstract This chapter examines the significant transformations within China's food sector since 1947. Initial policies, such as land reforms and the restructuring of rural production into communes, brigades and production teams, fundamentally altered China's rural production form. Some scholars believe that the rise in food output during this period can be attributed to the adoption of these new production forms and the "Dazhai" model of labour mobilisation. Additionally, from 1953, the state's stringent control over food procurement and retailing enabled the Maoist government to redistribute agricultural welfare and reallocate surplus from the food sector to urban industries. However, the effectiveness of these measures diminished as food output failed to keep pace with population growth, leading to a severe recession in agriculture under Mao's strict regime, which jeopardised China's food self-sufficiency. In 1979, Deng Xiaoping introduced reforms, beginning with the de-collectivisation of agriculture. This marked a stark departure from Maoist collective farming. Yet, the essential role of China's agriculture in supporting urban industry remained fundamentally unchanged.

Keywords Collectivisation • The state grain monopoly • Dazhai model • Rural collectives • Grain requisitioning and procurement • Great Leap Famine • De-collectivisation

J. Du, *Farmland, Farming and Food in the National Economy of China, 1947–2020*, Palgrave Studies in Economic History,
https://doi.org/10.1007/978-3-031-70027-9_1

The 1947 Land Reforms and Early Collectivisation

Due to the impact of the Second Sino-Japanese War (1939–1945 *di er ci zhong ri zhanzheng*)[1] and the subsequent Chinese Civil War[2] (1946–1949 *guogong neizhan*), China's agricultural performance significantly declined, reaching a crisis level by the eve of the founding of the People's Republic of China (PRC) in 1949. Compared to the pre-war year of 1936,[3] the country's agricultural gross domestic product GDP) in 1949 had decreased by one-fourth,[4] with per capita grain output at 209.0 kilogrammes.[5] At that time, 80% of the Chinese population experienced conditions of starvation or semi-starvation.[6]

With Mao's belief in the Soviet-led "world proletarian revolution" (*quan shijie wuchan jieji geming*), the Maoist regime naturally opposed the Western bloc. This opposition caused China's detachment from the US-led post-war international aid and trade systems. Given its large population size, the assistance that the Maoist government received from the Soviet Union was however inadequate to drive Chinese industrialisation. With the top priority placed on developing heavy industry, the Maoist government had little choice but to extract surpluses from the agricultural

[1] During World War II (*hereafter* WWII), the Second Sino-Japanese War unfolded between the Empire of Japan and the Republic of China from 1937 to 1945. This conflict notably inflicted severe economic detriment on the Chinese economy.

[2] The Chinese Civil War (1946–1949) was a pivotal conflict between the Kuomintang (KMT)-led Republic of China and the Chinese Communist Party (CCP). This war culminated in the CCP's rise to power on the Chinese mainland and the subsequent establishment of the PRC.

[3] According to Wu (2001), China's agricultural GDP was 14.5 billion yuan in 1936 calculated at the constant price level of that year. For detailed data and analysis on agricultural output during this period, refer to Wu, Chengming. *Modernization in China: Market and Society (Zhongguo de xiandaihua: shichang uu shehui)*. Beijing: SDX Joint Publishing Company, 2001.

[4] Sun, Jian. *Economic History of China: Modern Section, 1840–1949 (Zhongguo jingji shi: jindai bufen, 1840–1949 nian)*. Beijing: China Renmin University Press (Zhongguo renmin daxue chuban she), 1989.

[5] Information Office of the State Council of China. *Food Security in China (Zhongguo de liangshi Anquan)*. Government White Paper. Published October 2019. Http://www.scio.gov.cn/ztk/dtzt/39912/41906/index.htm. Accessed January 15, 2024a.

[6] Information Office of the State Council of China. *Grain Issues in China (Zhongguo de liangshi wenti)*. Government White Paper. Published in October 1996. Https://www.gov.cn/zhengce/2005-05/25/content_2615740.htm. Accessed January 15, 2024b.

sector,[7] mainly burdening the peasant class, and reallocating their surplus to urban industry.

However, the sluggish growth and occasional stagnation in China's post-war food sector not only impeded rural development but also posed a significant obstacle to Mao's ambitious goal of rapid industrialisation. It raised concerns about whether agricultural output could keep pace with population growth to adequately meet the needs of the populace.[8]

Thus, the post-war reconstruction in China began with agriculture, starting with the 1947 land reform. The "Outline of Land Law of China (*Zhongguo tudi fa dagang*),"[9] issued by the Chinese Communist Party (CCP) in 1947, outlined 16 key points, emphasising the implementation of the "land to the tillers" system[10] (*geng zhe you qi tian*) in Communist China. As articulated in the "Outline," landlordism was abolished, and all farmland was to be equitably redistributed among individual peasants, regardless of gender or age.

Subsequently, on September 29, 1949, the "Common Programme of the Chinese People's Political Consultative Conference (*Zhongguo renmin zhengzhi xieshang huiyi gongtong gangling*)"[11] outlined the CCP's nationwide objective of "transitioning feudal and semi-feudal land ownership into a system of peasant land ownership." These early land reforms officially recognised individual farmer's land property rights, significantly enhancing their incentives for agricultural production.

By 1952, the total grain output in China rose by 44.8% compared to 1949[12] (Fig. 1.1, Panel a), and per capita grain output had risen to 285.2 kilogrammes (Fig. 1.1, Panel b), reflecting a 36.5% increase from the 1949

[7] See Ash, Robert F. "Squeezing the Peasants: Grain Extraction, Food Consumption and Rural Living Standards in Mao's China." *The China Quarterly* 188 (2006): 959–998.

[8] A similar argument is presented by Barnett, Arthur Doak. *China's Economy in Global Perspective*. Washington: Brookings Institution, 1981.

[9] This legislation is also known as the 1947 "Basic Programme of the Agrarian Law" of China. For more detailed information, refer to the "Outline of Land Law of China" *(Zhongguo tudi fa dagang)*, published by the Central Committee of the CCP in Hebei on October 10, 1947.

[10] The full text of the 16 points outlined in the "Outline" can be found in Lee, Frank C. "Land Redistribution in Communist China." *Pacific Affairs* 21 (1948): 20–32.

[11] Chinese People's Political Consultative Conference. *Common Programme of the Chinese People's Political Consultative Conference (Zhongguo renmin zhengzhi xieshang huiyi gongtong gangling)*. Beijing: Chinese People's Political Consultative, September 29, 1949.

[12] In 1952, the total grain output reached 163.9 million tonnes, marking a significant rise from the 113.2 million tonnes recorded in 1949.

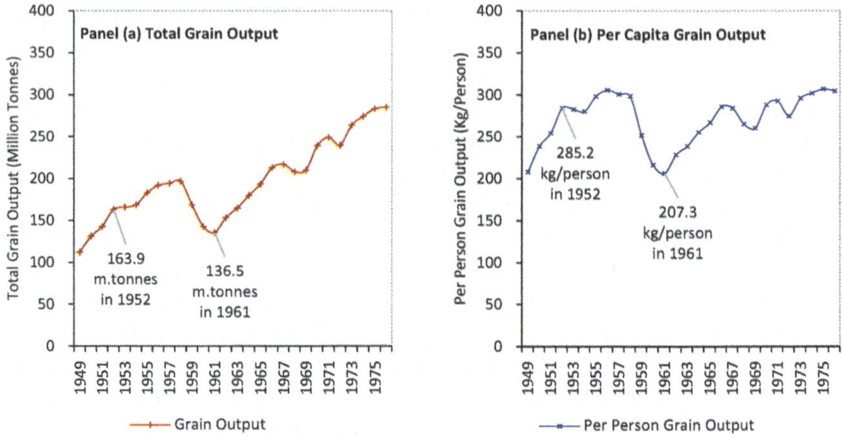

Fig. 1.1 Total grain output and per capita grain output in Mao's China

levels. This rapid improvement in rural productivity during the initial years of the PRC played a pivotal role in supporting its economic recovery. However, the onset of rural collectivisation, initiated in 1950, marked a shift away from the recently established system of private farmland ownership.

An essential factor contributing to this shift was the Korean War.[13] On the one hand, the industrial disparity between the United States and China during the "war to resist the United States and aid Korea (***kangmei yuanchao***)" prompted Mao's opinion to prioritise the heavy industry construction.[14] On the other, the Korean War, combined with the West Bloc's

[13] The Korean War, which erupted in June 1950 between North Korea and South Korea, ended with an armistice in July 1953. North Korea had strong support primarily from the former Soviet Union as well as China, while South Korea was mainly supported by the Western bloc, with the United States playing a leading role.

[14] China entered the Korean War in October 1950, deploying the People's Volunteer Army (*Zhongguo renmin zhiyuanjun*) to North Korea. The substantial gap in military capabilities led Mao to recognise China's limitations, highlighting the need to prioritise the advancement of heavy industry. Additionally, Mao's confidence in receiving technological assistance from the Soviet Union waned following Stalin's death. This shift promoted Mao to focus on developing an indigenous defence industry, emphasising the principle of self-reliance.

sanctions and trade embargo on China, compelled Mao to strengthen his diplomatic policy of "leaning-to-one-side" (*yi bian dao*) towards the Soviet-led Communist Bloc. With all relationships oriented solely towards the Soviet Union, Mao locked China's post-war construction into a complete Soviet-style socialist command model.

A direct result was the categorisation of the industry as the "priority sector" and agriculture as the "non-priority sector" to support China's industrialisation. Mao's directive was unequivocal: "use all possible means to squeeze out money to build (China's) heavy and defence industries."[15] Consequently, the government increased grain exports to finance its efforts in the "war to resist the United States." This period saw rapid expansion in domestic heavy industry construction, which resulted in an increase in the urban industrial population in China. In turn, this further intensified the Chinese government's requisitioning of grains.

In late 1951, the CCP Central Committee approved the "Resolution on Mutual Assistance and Collectivisation in Agricultural Production (Draft),"[16] officially marking the start of China's rural collectivisation drive.[17] This initiative was further endorsed by Mao's general lines for China's transition to socialism[18]: "Gradually achieve socialist industrialisation over a relatively long period of time, and gradually carry out socialist transformation in agriculture, handicrafts, and capitalist industry and commerce." As a result, the pace of rural collectivisation accelerated.

"In the initial years after the founding of the PRC, the Chinese government proactively engaged in societal food stock through grain

[15] For further insight into Mao's decision to develop China's heavy industry in the 1950s, refer to Mao, Zedong. *Collected Works of Mao Zedong*, Volume 6. Beijing: People's Publishing House (Renmin chuban she), 1951 [1992].

[16] Central Committee of the CCP. *Resolution of the Central Committee of the Communist Party of China on Mutual Assistance and Collectivisation in Agricultural Production (Draft) (Zhonggong zhongyang guanyu nongye shengchan huzhu hezuo de jueyi [cao an])*. Beijing: Central Committee of the CCP, December 15, 1951.

[17] While Mao advocated for rural collectives to "stick to the principles of voluntary participation and mutual benefit," the implementation often succumbed to local government commandism. This discrepancy made it challenging to fully realise the intended ideals.

[18] In the "general lines" policy, the transition from private land ownership to rural collectives was identified as one of the three major transformations (*san da gaizao*) that Mao's government sought to achieve during China's socialist transformation from 1953 to 1956.

requisitioning,"[19] supplemented by grain procurement (*gou liang*). From 1950 to 1953, the government's grain requisitioning remained relatively stable at approximately 14–15 million tonnes annually (Table 1.1, Column 1), which represented about 10% of the annual grain output. During this period, there was a noticeable increase in the state's procurement of grain, with figures rising from 4.5 million to 20.3 million tonnes in just three years (Table 1.1, Column 2). This led to the state's total grain requisitioning and procurement doubling between 1950 and 1953 (Table 1.1, Column 3). Despite this substantial increase, the effort fell short of fulfilling the escalating demand for grain, prompting the state to further intensify its grain possession strategies.

Table 1.1 Grain requisitioning (gong liang)[a] and procurement in 1950–1953

Year	*Agricultural tax Paid in grain (Million tonnes; %)*	*State's grain procurement (Million tonnes; %)*	*Grain requisitioning and procurement (Million tonnes; %)*
	(1)	(2)	(3) = (1) + (2)
1950	13.3 (10.1%)	4.5 (3.4%)	17.8 (13.5%)
1951	15.0 (10.4%)	9.0 (6.3%)	24.0 (16.7%)
1952	14.1 (8.6%)	15.7 (9.6%)	29.8 (18.2%)
1953	15.8 (9.5%)	20.3 (12.2%)	36.1 (21.7%)

Source: Grain requisitioning and procurement data was collected from Yang, Jisheng. "A Historical Review of the State Monopoly over Procurement and Retailing (Tonggou tongxiao de lishi huigu)." *Yanhuang Chunqiu* 12 (2008): 48–54

[a]Between 1951 and 1952, the ratio of grain requisitioning to procurement was 61:39, which later adjusted to 56:44. For a more comprehensive analysis, refer to Bo, Yibo. *Recollections on Certain Major Policies and Events (Ruogan zhong da juece yu shijian de huigu),* 2 volumes. Beijing: Central Party School Press (Zhonggong zhongyang dangxiao chubanshe), 1991: p. 258

[19] Grain requisitioning and procurement in China consisted of two main components: (1) the farming tax, paid in the form of food grain, and (2) the state's acquisition of grain from farmers for redistribution. After 1953, these practices were unified under the "state monopoly over procurement and retailing" (*tonggou tongxiao,* hereafter referred to as *the state grain monopoly*). This new system encompassed both planned and outside-plan purchases of grain from farmers by the state. This approach continued until 1985, when the government under Deng Xiaoping introduced a reform known as "contractual procurement" of grain (*hetong dinggou*).

State Grain Monopoly and Agricultural Collectivisation Drive

In 1953 and 1954, the government aimed to secure approximately 70 billion jin (35.0 million tonnes) of grain,[20] indicating that, beyond the "agricultural tax," an additional 21.6 million tonnes were required to fulfil the plan. This goal represented a 37.3% increase over the final procurement figure of 1952 (Table 1.1, Column 2). Primarily motivated by the need to finance warfare and industrialisation through the food sector, the government-set grain procurement prices substantially lower—by "20 to 30 per cent"[21]—than market rates. This discrepancy posed significant challenges for meeting the grain procurement targets, ultimately leading to a grain procurement crisis in 1953.[22]

In response to these challenges, Chen Yun[23] proposed a solution to Mao in October 1953: the implementation of a state monopoly over grain procurement and retailing.[24] By November, the Chinese government's administrative council officially adopted this "state grain monopoly" system,[25] marking the beginning of a decades-long period of closed grain

[20] Ibid.

[21] Ibid.

[22] The 1953 grain crisis was fundamentally a crisis of grain procurement. Key explanations for this crisis include: (1) competition from private grain traders undermining state efforts in the grain market; (2) farmers' preference to hold onto surplus grain; (3) a general disincentive among small-scale farmers and peasants due to the inherent conflict between the focus on developing heavy industry and the needs of agriculture, among other factors. For a more detailed examination of the 1953 grain crisis, refer to Tian, Xiquan. "The Grain Crisis, the General Line for the Transitional Period and the Promulgation of the Policy for Unified Purchase and Sale of Grain (1953 nian liangshi weiji yu tonggou tongxiao zhengce de chutai)." *Journal of East China Normal University (Philosophy and Social Sciences) (Huadong shifan daxue xuebao [zhexue shehui kexue ban])* 39 (2007): 54–60.

[23] Chen Yun (1905–1995), who served as the secretary of the Secretariat of the CCP Central Committee in 1953, was a pivotal figure within the core leadership of the CCP, significantly influencing China's economic policy-making.

[24] The "*tonggou tongxiao*" system, a state monopoly established to resolve the grain procurement difficulties faced in 1953, was formally known as "*nong chanpin tonggou tongxiao*," which translates to the state monopoly over the procurement and retailing of agricultural products. This system encompassed a wide range of agricultural goods, including most grain crops, cotton, oil seeds, among others. It facilitated the state's acquisition of rural surplus and significantly distorted China's agricultural production patterns, skewing them towards the state's requisition needs for urban industries.

[25] Government Administrative Council of the Central People's Government of China. *Decree on Planned Procurement and Planned Supply of Food Grain (Guanyu shixing liangshi de jihua shougou he jihua gongying de mingling)*. Beijing: The Government Administration Council of the Central People's Government of China, November 19, 1953.

circulation. Under this system, grain producers were obligated to meet allocated planned procurement quotas and sell surplus grain at government-set prices. This approach heavily favoured heavy industrial construction at the expense of the food sector by squeezing surplus from rural producers.[26]

In the initial year (1954–1955) following the introduction of the "state grain monopoly system," the government requisitioned 53.9 billion jin of food grains, a 7.5% increase from the previous year.[27] Evidently, this discrepancy suggests that the increase in requisitioning was primarily sourced from rural surplus grains. The government's additional extraction of surplus food grains discouraged farmers from both selling and producing more. The only viable solution was a gradual shift towards deeper rural collectivisation (see Table 1.2).

Table 1.2 Collectivisation in agriculture, 1950–1958

	Total (%)	*Agricultural mutual aid team (%)*	*Agricultural collectives (%)*	*People's commune (%)*
	(1)	(2)	(3)	(4)
1950	10.7	10.7	–	–
1951	19.2	19.2	–	–
1952	40.0	39.9	0.1	–
1953	39.5	39.3	0.2	–
1954	60.3	58.3	2.0	–
1955	64.9	50.7	14.2	–
1956	97.2	0.9	96.3	–
1957	97.5	–	97.5	–
1958	99.1	–		99.1

Source: Office of Agricultural Statistics, National Bureau of Statistics of China. ***Brilliant Accomplishments of China's Agriculture 1949–1984 (Zhongguo nongye de guanghui chengjiu 1949–1984)***. Beijing: China Statistics Press (Zhongguo tongji chuban she), 1984

[26] For details, refer to Ash, Robert F. "Squeezing the Peasants: Grain Extraction, Food Consumption and Rural Living Standards in Mao's China." *The China Quarterly 188* (2006): 959–998.

[27] For detailed data on grain requisitioning after the implementation of the "state grain monopoly," refer to Yang, Jisheng. "A Historical Review of the State Monopoly over Procurement and Retailing (Tonggou tongxiao de lishi huigu)." *Yanhuang Chunqiu* 12 (2008): 48–54, Table 3.

At the farm gate level, interacting with rural collectives proved to be more feasible for the state than managing 510 million individual farmers.[28] Consequently, as China's agriculture transitioned from basic to advanced production collectives, the transaction costs associated with the state grain monopoly decreased markedly, owing to the "efficiency" of the new form of production. Within four years, from 1953 to 1957, agricultural collectives were established across China. This expansion led to a dramatic rise in the percentage of farmers participating in collectives, from 39.5% to 97.5% (Table 1.2, Column 3). Concurrently, all farmland acquired by farmers during the land reforms was reintegrated into collective ownership.

While it remains inconclusive whether industrial growth during the recovery period of the early 1950s compensated for the loss experienced by peasants and their surpluses,[29] it is clear that the standard of living in China at the time fell to barely subsistent levels.[30] The food sector had little left for further extraction. Then, a critical question for the Mao government was to identify a balanced and optimal level of "squeezing" that would neither excessively impede industrial growth nor undermine peasants' long-term production incentives. To transform the food sector into a source of surplus transfer, the Mao government employed two key instruments.

- **Collectivisation:** The first instrument was collectivisation, which transformed individual household-based rural production form into state-controlled "rural collectives." This instrument imposed an institutional framework for facilitating large-scale welfare transfers orchestrated by the CCP. However, this centralised top-down system stripped peasants of any decision-making authority about crop

[28] In 1953, the total rural population was 509.7 million. For more information, refer to the National Bureau of Statistics of China. National Data. Https://data.stats.gov.cn/english/easyquery.htm. Accessed January 15, 2024.

[29] See Ash, Robert F., Jane Du, and Cheng King. "Perspectives on Agricultural and Grain Output Growth in China from the Nineteenth Century to the Present Day." In Pinilla, V. and H. Willebald (eds.). *Agricultural Development in the World Periphery: A Global Economic History Approach*. London: Palgrave Macmillan, 2018.

[30] For a detailed discussion on the living standards in China during this period, consult the work by Allen, Robert C. *Global Economic History: A Very Short Introduction*. Oxford: Oxford University Press, 2011; and Allen, Robert C., Jean-Pascal Bassino, Debin Ma, Christine Moll-Murata, and Jan Luiten van Zanden. "Wages, Prices, and Living Standards in China, 1739–1925: In Comparison with Europe, Japan, and India." *Economic History Review* 64 (2011): 8–38.

planting, thereby diminishing their motivation to optimise land productivity.

- **State grain monopoly:** The second instrument employed by the Mao government was the state grain monopoly. This monopoly system replaced all existing agricultural product markets with a state-manipulated distribution network. By implementing this system, the Mao government effectively severed all direct connections between peasants and the markets, thereby creating a nationwide network that facilitated the extraction and redirection of rural surpluses from agriculture to meet the government's requirements for political rent extraction.

These two institutional changes fundamentally transformed the rural structure and production forms. Basic economic functions were restricted or even entirely stripped from rural households. The state grain monopoly completely isolated peasants from the product market, disconnecting them from any direct involvement in or benefits from market dynamics. Meanwhile, collectivisation reduced the effort levels among participants in collective farms and transferred decision-making authority from individual household to the state apparatus. This centralised control over food production decisions symbolised a drastic departure from traditional, household-based agricultural practices.

Great Leap Forward and People's Commune

After the Korean War ended in 1953, the central government's focus shifted back to domestic economic construction. The transplantation of the command economic system in China began to reveal its limitations during the First Five-Year Plan (1953–1957). The imitated Soviet-style economic policies had created serious imbalances in the Chinese economy.[31] Against this backdrop, Mao urged the nation to "draw lessons from

[31] Soviet-styled economic policies are considered to have created an imbalanced economy in China, where the "non-priority" sector had to compete with the "priority" sector for resources and scarcities. This let to imbalanced demand-supply relationships in many aspects of the macroeconomy, including wage goods and raw materials. For details, refer to Lin, Justin Y. "Inflation and Growth in China's Transition: A Comparison with Eastern Europe and the Former Soviet Union." In Guitian, Manuel, and Robert A. Mundell (eds.). *Inflation and Growth in China: Proceedings of a Conference Held in Beijing, China, May 10–12, 1995*. Washington: International Monetary Fund, 1996. Https://www.elibrary.imf.org/display/book/9781557755421/ch015.xml. Accessed January 15, 2024.

the Soviet Union" (*yi su wei jian*) and proposed ideas better suited to China's conditions for socialist construction in his "On the Ten Major Relationships (*lun shi da guanxi*)."[32] Subsequently, the CCP Eighth National Congress began adjusting the economic structure to achieve a comprehensive balance steadily and progressively, aiming for a strategy that was neither "conservative" (*bao shou*) nor "adventurous" (*mao jin*).

However, in the face of the "socialist high tide"[33] in production towards the end of 1955, Mao shifted his approach from steady socialist construction to one that sought to "continuously break the balance"[34] during transitional period. With the First Five-Year Plan completed ahead of schedule, Mao began to believe that "anti-adventurism" (*fan mao jin*) had constrained the enthusiasm of the masses. He argued that China should adopt unconventional methods to overcome the deadlock in its socialist construction.

Following Mao's visit to the former Soviet Union, in early 1958, he introduced the policy of "surpassing Britain and catching up with America" (*chao ying gan mei*). Later, in May 1958, Mao's "general line for socialist construction"[35] was formally endorsed at the Second Session of the Eighth CCP National Congress. This directive emphasised China's imperative to exert maximum effort, strive for a leading position, and expedite the construction of socialism more efficiently and economically.

While the industrial sector focused solely on steel production, Mao advocated for China's agriculture to "take food grain as the key link (*yi liang wei gang*)." At the same time, the 12-year rural development plan was drastically shortened, with goals set to be completed in just two to

[32] Mao, Zedong. *Selected Works of Mao Tse-Tung*, Volume V. Beijing: People's Publishing House (Renmin chuban she), 1977 [2014].

[33] Walker, Kenneth R. "Collectivisation in Retrospect: The 'Socialist High Tide' of Autumn 1955–Spring 1956." *The China Quarterly* 26 (1966): 1–43.

[34] Liu Shaoqi quoted Mao's thoughts on "breaking the balance" to instruct work during the transitional period at an informal meeting held in December 1955. For more details, refer to Bo, Yibo. *Recollections on Certain Major Policies and Events (Ruogan zhong da juece yu shijian de huigu)*, 2 volumes. Beijing: Central Party School Press (Zhonggong zhongyang dangxiao chubanshe), 1991: p. 522.

[35] Mao's general line directing the Chinese people during the socialist construction era was characterised by an ambitious ethos: "going all out, aiming high, and achieving greater, faster, better, and more economical results in building socialism (*Gu zu ganjing, lizheng shangyou, duo kuai hao sheng de jianshe shehui zhuyi*)." This approach received formal endorsement at the Second Session of the Eighth CCP National Congress.

three years.[36] In pursuit of the "general line," Mao initiated the Great Leap Forward (*da yue jin*) in 1958.

During the Great Leap Forward, most local governments disseminated inflated grain output reports, portraying them as "satellites"[37] that purportedly demonstrated the superiority of China's socialist food sector. Various practices in grain production, including "rice satellites," "wheat satellites," "tobacco satellites," "maize satellites" (*yu mi*) and others, were collectively designated as "Launching Satellite" (*fang wei xing*).[38]

- On June 8th, 1958, the *People's Daily* (*renmin ribao*) stated that the Weixing Collective in Suiping, Henan, had successfully launched its first "satellite," with wheat yields reaching an average of 2105 jin per mu.[39]
- Following this, the *China Youth Daily* (*Zhongguo qingnian bao*) published a commentary by Qian Xuesen,[40] in which he suggested that China's grain yield could potentially achieve as high as 40,000 jin per mu.[41]

[36] Mao, Zedong. *Mao Zedong's Manuscripts Since the Founding of the State (Jianguo yilai Mao Zedong wengao)*, volume 7. Beijing: Central Literature Publishing House (Zhongyang wenxian chuban she), 1958 [1992].

[37] In 1957, the Soviet Union achieved a historic achievement by launching the world's first artificial satellite, significantly enhancing its prestige. This scientific triumph was not only a matter of national pride but also became a symbol of accomplishment for the socialist camp, highlighting the advanced techniques and achievements that underscored the superiority of socialism. Over the subsequent years, the term "satellite" evolved beyond its literal meaning to become an iconic symbol within this context. For more details, refer to Du, Jun. *Agricultural Transition in China: Domestic and International Perspectives on Technology and Institutional Change*. Basingstoke: Palgrave Macmillan, 2018.

[38] Notably, among these symbolic satellites, the "wheat satellites" and "rice satellites" stood out for their particular significance.

[39] The reported yield of 2105 *jin* per mu translates to an impressive 15.8 tonnes per hectare. This figure starkly contrasts with the national wheat yield in 1957, which, according to the National Bureau of Statistics, was 0.9 tonnes per hectare. For more data, refer to National Bureau of Statistics of China. National Data. Https://data.stats.gov.cn/english/easyquery.htm. Accessed January 15, 2024.

[40] Qian, Xuesen. "How Much Grain Yield per Mu? (Liangshi muchan liang huiyou duoshao)." *China Youth Daily (Zhongguo qingnian bao)*, published on June 16, 1958: p. 4.

[41] A yield of 4353 jin per mu is equivalent to approximately 300 tonnes per hectare. In comparison, the 1958 wheat yield in the United States was approximately 1.9 tonnes per hectare. This data was collected from the United States Department of Agriculture. National Agricultural Statistics Services. Http://www.nass.usda.gov. Accessed January 15, 2024.

- Inspired by the Weixing Collective's success, local governments initiated their own "satellites." On June 12th, 1958, the *People's Daily* reported another "satellite" launched by the same Weixing Producer's Collective, with wheat yields reaching 3530 jin per mu.[42]
- On June 16th, 1958, Xinhua News Agency reported that the Wang Mingjin experimental farmland in the Xingguang Collective in Gucheng County, Hubei Province, had surpassed the previous wheat yield record, achieving a yield of 4353 jin per *mu*.
- Subsequently, on June 23rd, the Xianfeng Collective, also in Gucheng, reported an increased yield to 4689 jin per mu.
- By July 12th, the Heping Collective of Chengguan Township in Xiping County, Henan Province, was featured in the *People's Daily* for setting a new record with their wheat field, reaching an unprecedented yield of 7320 jin per mu.
- On August 13th, the Xijianyuan No. 1 Collective in Macheng County, Hubei Province, announced through Xinhua News Agency that they had achieved a rice yield of 36,900 jin per mu.[43]
- This series of announcements highlighted rapidly escalating grain yields per mu. On September 25th, 1958, the highest recorded wheat yield in China reached 8586 jin per mu,[44] achieved by the Saishike area in the Qaidam Basin, Qinghai.
- Moreover, the highest rice yield was achieved by the Hongqi People's Commune of Huanjiang County in Jiangxi Province, which announced a staggering yield of 130,435 jin per mu.[45]

The optimistic projections for grain production in 1958 led to a misguided belief that food problem had been resolved. This illusion shifted the CCP's focus towards industrial development, with a primary emphasis on steel production.[46] The Great Leap Forward's push into China's heavy industry began in September 1958.

[42] This figure was calculated based on data from a 2.9 mu experimental wheat field.

[43] The rice yield of 36,900 jin per mu translates to 276.8 tonnes per hectare, according to reports by Chinese media. To celebrate the advancements in agricultural technology, often referred to as "Satellites," a series of films and documentaries were produced. Notable examples include "Boiling Guangxi" (*feiteng de Guangxi*) and "Harvest Song" (*fengshou qu*).

[44] This is about 64.4 tonnes per hectare.

[45] This is about 978.3 tonnes per hectare.

[46] Bo, Yibo. *Recollections on Certain Major Policies and Events (Ruogan zhong da juece yu shijian de huigu),* 2 volumes. Beijing: Central Party School Press (Zhonggong zhongyang dangxiao chubanshe), 1991: p. 690.

Indeed, even before the Great Leap Forward, the construction of water conservancy infrastructure in 1957 had diverted a substantial workforce away from grain production. It was asserted that in 1958, "over 60 million rural labourers" were redirected towards "small-scale, local, and group (*xiao tu qun*)" industrial production.[47] This number further increased during the Great Leap Forward.

The ambitious 1958 "Launching Satellite" campaign and the depletion of agricultural labour eventually led to catastrophic consequences for grain output. The Chinese government made ultimately unrealistic claims about enhanced grain output. Just a few months after asserting that China's rice and wheat yields had reached historical highs, the "Great Leap Famine" (*da ji huang*) began.[48]

Communism, Communalisation and Great Leap Famine

At the same time as the "Launching Satellite" campaign, rural collectivisation reached its zenith alongside communisation. By the end of 1958, as shown in Table 1.2, 99.1% of rural farmers had been organised into people's communes. China's agricultural sector and rural farming underwent a profound shift towards large-scale collective production. However, the diversion of rural labourers away from farming, diminished incentives due to collectivisation and communisation, and the impairment of farming tools during the "large-scale steelmaking (*da lian gang tie*)" collectively led to a substantial decline in rural productivity. In response, the Party Central Committee prioritised grain procurement in 1958 to ensure food supplies for workers in urban factories and residents in the cities. Consequently, actual grain requisitioning in 1958 exceeded that of 1957.

Mao thus believed that rural China was not facing a food shortage; rather, he thought that farmers were underreporting grain output to hoard for personal use.[49] Subsequently, the government intensified its

[47] Ibid, p. 708.

[48] From an economic viewpoint, the Great Leap Forward's restriction on farmers' rights to leave rural collectives in 1959 can be seen as a catalyst for the abrupt decline in rural productivity during the People's Commune period. The persistent downturn in productivity was a primary factor leading to the Great Leap Famine. For further insight, consult Lin, Justin Y. "Collectivization and China's Agricultural Crisis in 1959–1961." *Journal of Political Economy* 98 (1990): 1228–1252.

[49] In February 1959, the Guangdong Provincial Party Committee reported an issue in Leinan County involving the concealment of agricultural output, revealing that approximately 70 million *jin* of grain had been discovered concealed.

control over the grain procurement system through a nationwide anti-concealment campaign, which further suppressed grain output.

Beyond its immediate impacts, rural collectivisation fundamentally altered the social status of the Chinese peasant class. The establishment of rural communes and brigades, which took over decision-making of plantations from peasants, seriously disrupted the technological advancements that had previously dominated food crop production. It is widely acknowledged that the rural collectivisation of the 1950s facilitated the Mao government to systemically squeeze and reallocate surplus from the food sector to subsidise industrialisation,[50] which significantly deteriorated the well-being of peasants. Moreover, this shift in the peasant's role in the economy contributed to the entrenchment of the rural-urban dichotomy in Chinese society, marking a long-lasting alteration in China's socio-economic environment.

At the farm gate, the structure of plantations before collectivisation was characterised by the cultivation of "low-value" food crop varieties. This gradually shifted into "high-value" grain crop production, with a focus on rice and wheat.[51] Despite the reforms implemented by Deng Xiaoping and Liu Shaoqi to overturn some policies from the Great Leap Forward, food policies largely remained untouched. Considering that, for most years from the start of collectivisation until the opening-up reforms, per capita food output was actually lower than in the pre-collectivisation period,[52] the only rationale behind the change in plantation becomes clear—central

[50] For a more detailed discussion on squeezing the food sector to subsidise industrialisation, see the following works: Ash, Robert F. "Squeezing the Peasants: Grain Extraction, Food Consumption and Rural Living Standards in Mao's China." *The China Quarterly* 188 (2006): 959–998; Lardy, Nicholas R. *Agriculture in China's Modern Economic Development*. Cambridge: Cambridge University Press, 1983; and Lyons, Thomas P. "Feeding Fujian: Grain Production and Trade, 1986–1996." *The China Quarterly* 155 (1998): 512–545.

[51] From 1955 to 1960, rural collectivisation quickly increased the acreage of rice and wheat from 37.0% to 37.8% of China's total sown area. This figure slightly decreased to about 36.2% when the Chinese state eased its control over wheat and rice cultivation in 1961–1962. Since then, the acreage for these crops increased monotonically until the Dengist economic reforms. By 1980, the combined share of rice and wheat accounted for 42.9% of the total annual total sown area, according to data from the National Bureau of Statistics of China. National Data. Https://data.stats.gov.cn/english/easyquery.htm. Accessed January 15, 2024.

[52] In 1952, China's per capita grain production reached 285.2 kilogrammes per person per year. By 1961, this figure had decreased to 207.3 kilogrammes. This data was retrieved from the National Bureau of Statistics of China. National Data. Https://data.stats.gov.cn/english/easyquery.htm. Accessed January 15, 2024.

planners aimed to increase the government's ability to extract surplus rice and wheat from China's food sector.

The consolidation of agricultural production into people's communes and brigades significantly lowered the production incentives for peasants. Meanwhile, the massive extraction of rural labour from agriculture to steel production during the Great Leap Forward drastically reduced food output. This reduction in food output, coupled with the state's policy failures, resulted in a severe food shortage across China, particularly affecting rural areas. When the situation was worsened with three consecutive years of natural disasters from 1959 to 1961, Mao's collectivisation and Great Leap Forward culminated in the devastating "Great Leap Famine."[53] In January 1962, the Central Committee of the CCP scrutinised the leftist errors in grain management at the "7,000 Cadres Conference (*qiqian ren dahui*)" to address the famine and food shortages.

Official population statistics indicate a significant decrease during the years 1959–1962. In 1959, the Chinese population totalled 672.1 million,[54] falling to 662.1 million in 1960, and further to 658.6 million in 1961, reflecting a reduction of 13.5 million within just two years. Many observers have questioned the reliability and accuracy of these official figures. Considering birth rates and natural population growth, it is

[53] China's Great Leap Famine is recognised as the deadliest famine in human history and the most severe famine of the modern era. Due to the constraints imposed by the unavailability of archival sources, accurately assessing the mortality rate has been challenging. Estimates of the death toll range from 20 million to 60 million with a common estimate approximately 30 million deaths. However, Frank Dikötter, after four years of extensive research, contends that the death toll may have reached as high as 45 million. This figure is close to estimates by Chinese official Chen Yizi, who stated in an interview with Jasper Becker that the toll was between 43 million and 46 million. Yang Jisheng has mentioned a similar figure of 36 million. Chinese demographer Peng Xizhe and historian Cao Shuji have estimated 22 million and 32.5 million deaths, respectively, during the Great Leap Famine. For a more comprehensive understanding, recommended readings include: Cao, Shuji. "The Deaths of China's Population and Its Root Cause during 1959–1961 (1959–1961 nian Zhongguo de renkou siwang ji qi chengyin)." *Chinese Journal of Population Science (Zhongguo renkou kexue)* 1 (2005): 14–28; Dikötter, Frank. *Mao's Great Famine: The History of Chinas Most Devastating Catastrophe, 1958–1962*. London: Bloomsbury, 2010; Peng, Xizhe. "Demogrpahic Consequences of the Great Leap Forward in China's Provinces." *Population and Development Review* 13 (1987): 639–670; Yang, Jisheng. *Tombstone: The Untold Story of Mao's Great Famine*. London: Allen Lane, 2012; Becker, Jasper. *Hungry Ghosts: China's Secret Famine*. London: John Murray, 1996.

[54] National Bureau of Statistics of China. National Data. Https://data.stats.gov.cn/english/easyquery.htm. Accessed January 15, 2024.

suggested that there were likely a substantial number of "abnormal deaths," potentially in tens of millions, during the famine. The essence of Mao's policy of "rushing into communism (*paobu jinru gongchan zhuyi*)" was manifested in the reliance on agriculture for industrial accumulation. The change in planation structure to favour the government's preferred crop composition came at a significant cost, which was not borne by the Chinese state. Instead, Chinese peasants and the broader food sector disproportionately shouldered the burden and cost.

Mao's Ideology in Agricultural Policy–Making

Soviet-style industrialisation prioritised heavy industry. Unlike the Soviet Union, China lacked a strong economic foundation for developing heavy industry in the early years following its establishment. Due to the absence of basic capital stock, China's initial industrial accumulation had to rely on its agricultural sector.

However, China's agriculture was traditionally based on small-scale farming. Land reforms from 1947 to 1952 further decentralised agricultural production by redistributing farmland from landowners equally among individual peasants, making the small-scale peasant economy even more prevalent. The significant gap between the limited farming surplus and the demands of heavy industry implied that China's initial capital accumulation for heavy industry could take an extended period, posing a challenge to Mao's aspiration for "leaping into communism." In this context, the small-scale peasant economy was perceived as a natural contradiction to early industrial development. Consequently, in its pursuit of rapid industrialisation, the Mao government inevitably neglected the rural-urban balance.

The state grain monopoly system was thereby introduced to address the contractionary intersectoral imbalance and facilitate government control over the grain sector. On the supply side, Mao implemented a compulsory procurement system to secure the majority of agricultural output for urban redistribution. On the demand side, a commodity ration coupon system was established in the 1950s to manage the planned urban distribution of scarce products. Among these, the food coupon (*liang piao*)[55] system was

[55] To coordinate the state grain monopoly system with planned grain circulation and distribution, the Mao government implemented a "four certificates, three coupons" system (*si zheng san piao*). The four certificates included certificates for urban food grain consumption,

particularly important in completing the closed circle of the state grain monopoly.

In addition, agricultural collectivisation further reduced transaction cost associated with state requisitioning. Subsequently, the People's Commune system ultimately opened channels for the Mao government to maximise the transfer of farming surplus to urban industry. In the years that followed, agricultural production strategically positioned in Mao vision for China's socialist construction, encapsulated in his overarching idea about agricultural issues—"taking food grains as the key link."[56] This principle resulted in the diversion of a substantial proportion of the grain surplus away from agriculture, creating disincentives for farmers. Traditionally, China's agriculture had been labour-intensive. Therefore, before the implementation of land- and labour-saving technological advancements implemented in the 1980s, inefficiencies in the food sector were widespread across China.

From 1952 to 1960, the industrial sector's contribution to GDP increased by 23.6% (Fig. 1.2, Panel a). Towards the end of 1970s, this figure had surged to as high as 47.7%, according to official data, a level significantly higher than in most other developing countries of the time. In contrast, the industrial share in total employment remained almost unchanged, rising by only 11.3%[57] (Fig. 1.2, Panel d). This would have

urban food grain transfer, industrial and commercial grain use, and urban and township fodder grain use. The three coupons were for national and local level food grain consumption, and for local fodder grain consumption. Here, food coupons specifically refer to those used for urban food grain consumption, which were abolished in the 1993 food system reform.

[56] During the Great Leap Forward, Mao emphasised that "the key link" in agriculture was grain, while in industry was steel. This principle was frequently mentioned in Mao's work instructions during Central Committee meetings and was formally endorsed in a document issued by CCP Central Committee in 1960. For details, refer to Bo, Yibo. *Recollections on Certain Major Policies and Events (Ruogan zhong da juece yu shijian de huigu)*, 2 volumes. Beijing: Central Party School Press (Zhonggong zhongyang dangxiao chubanshe), 1991: p. 698; and Central Committee of the Chinese Communist Party. *Zhonggong zhongyang zhuanfa nongye bu dangzu "guanyu quanguo nongye gongzuo huiyi de baogao" (Circular of the Central Committee on the "Report on the National Agricultural Work Conference" Issued by the Party Leadership Group of the Ministry of Agriculture)*. Beijing: Chinese Communist Party Central Committee, March 19, 1960.

[57] The share of national employment in the secondary industry rose significantly, increasing from 8.1% in 1952 to 19.5% by 1960.

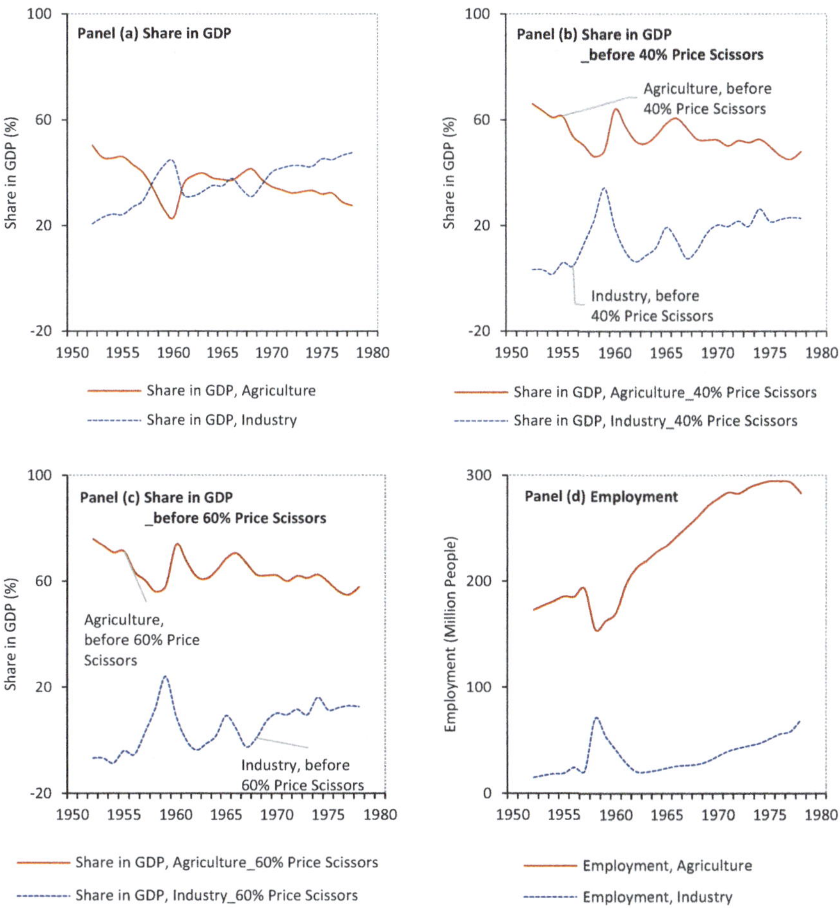

Fig. 1.2 Share of industry in national employment and GDP in Mao's China, before and after price scissors

only implied that significant labour-saving technology changes occurred in the industrial sector under Mao's central planning system.

However, this disparity in fact stems from the intersectoral wealth reallocation through price scissors, which was further exacerbated during the Great Leap Forward. When adjusted for the 40% (Fig. 1.2, Panel b) and

60% (Fig. 1.2, Panel c) intersectoral price distortions,[58] the trend in industrial sector employment more closely mirrored its GDP contribution. The rationale behind this was the Mao government's aim to maximise the acquisition of low-priced agricultural products from rural China to keep urban wage costs low, thereby accelerating capital accumulation through intersectoral price manipulation.

In this context, industrial output was largely overestimated, while agriculture's contribution to national income was significantly underestimated. After accounting for scissor pricing, the average industrial share of national GDP deflated to as low as 20%[59] to 30% (Fig. 1.2, Panel c).

Together with the Household Registration System (*hu kou*) and the urban *food coupon system*, the state grain monopoly system created a clear division between the agricultural and industrial sectors in China. This division has resulted in the rural-urban dualistic structure, which remains a crucial contradiction in the socio-economic development of contemporary China. This dualistic structure is likely to persist as a constraint on the sustainability of economic growth.

Since 1949, the transformations in the food sector have been comprehensive. Early initiatives, such as land reforms and the restructuring of rural production into communes, brigades and production teams, fundamentally altered rural production forms.[60] Additionally, the government's

[58] "Price scissors" system refers to an intersectoral arbitrage executed by the Maoist government to extract resources and surplus from the peasantry to support industrial expansion through intersectoral price distortion. It is estimated that from 1953 to 1978, 17% of the national income from China's agricultural sector was reallocated to industry through the price scissors system. Including the agricultural tax, this share could reach up to 22.4%, creating an intersectoral gap amounting to 44.5% of the national income. To illustrate the real intersectoral composition of the Chinese economy, Fig. 1.2, Panels b and c, plots the estimated share of agricultural and industrial production in GDP before the 40–60% welfare allocation. For more information on price manipulation and the price gap before the Dengist reforms, see Wu, Li. "Dialectic Discussion on the Price Gap in China's 'Price Scissors' from 1949 to 1978 (1949–1978 nian zhongguo 'jian dao cha' cha'e bianzheng)." *Researches in Chinese Economic History (Zhongguo jingji shi yanjiu)* 4 (2001): 3–12.

[59] For detailed discussion on industrial growth during the Mao era, please refer to Deng, Keng, Jim H. Shen, and Jingyuan Guo. "Performance and Mechanisms of the Maoist Economy—A Holistic Approach, 1950–1980." *Journal of the Economic and Social History of the Orient* (2024): forthcoming. Http://eprints.lse.ac.uk/124262. Accessed August 30, 2024.

[60] The reforms related to land and land-based production in China are recognised for their far-reaching impact on agricultural output and productivity. Their significance extends beyond mere "temporary improvements in its immediate aftermath as the destruction of

stringent monopoly over food procurement and retailing, established in 1953,[61] enabled the redistribution of agricultural welfare and the reallocation of surplus from the food sector to urban industries. Despite the setbacks during the Great Leap Famine (1959–1961), these fundamental changes in rural institutions, combined with the reorganisation of rural production and increased labour output, significantly enhanced China's agricultural performance.

Some scholars attribute the increase in food output during the Maoist era to the adoption of new forms of organisation[62] by collectives and communes, as well as the Dazhai movement, which involved extensive labour mobilisation with only small-scale technical changes.[63] This

'feudal exploitations', ..., to the final achievement of what can be considered the Chinese equivalent of a Green Revolution." For a comprehensive examination of land reform and its influence on rural production, refer to Wong, John. *Land Reform in the People's Republic of China*. New York: Praeger, 1973.

[61] The introduction of a state grain monopoly in the 1950s marked a pivotal economic planning policy aimed at regulating agricultural output and resource allocation. Initiated in 1953, the Chinese government implemented grain procurement plans targeted at the food sector and enforced a quantitative rationing system within urban industries. This policy facilitated the redistribution of rural welfare towards the urban sector, bolstering China's industrialisation efforts. Critics argue that such policies resulted in severe exploitation of both Chinese peasants and urban workers, persisting until the policy's formal repeal in the 1990s. For an in-depth look at the enactment of this policy, refer to Government Administrative Council of the Central People's Government of China. *Decree on Planned Procurement and Planned Supply of Food Grain (Guanyu shixing liangshi de jihua shougou he jihua gongying de mingling)*. Beijing: Government Administration Council of the Central People's Government of China, November 19, 1953.

[62] Many scholars argue that the early stages of rural reconstruction in China introduced new production forms that fundamentally restructured agricultural production. This reorganisation resulted in a significant increase in food output, primarily through the intensification of labour input. For more in-depth research on this topic, refer to Ishikawa, Shigeru. "Resource Flow between Agriculture and Industry—The Chinese Experience." *The Developing Economies* 5 (1967): 3–49; Walker, Kenneth R. "Organization for Agricultural Production." In Eckstein, Alexander, Walter Galenson, and Ta-Chung Liu (eds.). *Economic Trends in Communist China*. Edinburgh: Edinburgh University Press, 1968; Zweig, David. *Agrarian Radicalism in China, 1968–1981*. Cambridge, Massachusetts and London: Harvard University Press, 1989.

[63] In research exploring the technical transformation during the initial phases of agricultural development, significant emphasis was placed on changes in inputs and the planning programmes. For details, please refer to Kuo, Leslie Tse-Chiu. *The Technical Transformation of Agriculture in Communist China*. New York: Praeger Press, 1972; and Vermeer, Eduard B. *Water Conservancy and Irrigation in China: Social, Economic and Agrotechnical Aspects*. Leiden: Leiden University Press, 1977.

suggests that food output under Maoism was largely a result of labour intensification. Nonetheless, even if this was the case, the effectiveness of these techniques and institutions had waned.[64] Throughout the 1960s and 1970s, China's food output struggled to keep pace with its growing population.

Meanwhile, Mao's "food mismanagement"[65] had resulted in a downturn in the food sector, which jeopardised national food sufficiency. Between 1976 and 1978, just before the opening-up reform, China's domestic food deficits reached levels comparable to those before the Great Leap Famine (Table 1.3, Column 1). Any further decline in this system could have worsened the food shortage. The restoration of agriculture, after being mismanaged under the Maoist policies, necessitated fundamental changes.

In 1979, Deng Xiaoping embarked on economic reforms, beginning with the de-collectivisation of agriculture. This marked a complete departure from Maoist collective production, transitioning rural production back to a household-based model, reminiscent of the initial years after the creation of the PRC. However, the fundamental role of agriculture in supporting urban industry remained largely unchanged.

Data Analysis and Problems with Official Statistics

An inevitable and controversial issue in research on the Chinese economy is the accuracy of official statistical data. It has been widely argued that data from the National Bureau of Statistics can be disputable and lack reliability. This problem was particularly significant in research on Mao's China. Following Deng Xiaoping opening of the Chinese economy to the world, a new challenge emerged: overhauling China's statistical system to track a market-oriented economy, making accurate accounting of economic activities during the transformation increasingly difficult.

[64] Perkins, Dwight H. (ed.). *China's Modern Economy in Historical Perspective.* Stanford: Stanford University Press, 1975.

[65] See, Ryan, James. *Lenin's Terror, the Ideological Origin of Early Soviet State Violence.* London: Routledge, 2012.

Table 1.3 Domestic food deficits in Mao's China

	Food deficit (Million tonnes)
1953–1955	8.9
1956–1960	14.8
1961–1965	−13.4
1966–1970	1.5
1971–1975	−2.1
1976–1978	−11.3

Notes: Negative figures mean food imports were necessary to bridge domestic food deficits

Source: Contemporary Agricultural History Research Office, Rural Economic Research Centre, Ministry of Agriculture (eds.). *A Study of Agricultural Reforms and Development in Contemporary China (Dangdai Zhongguo nongye biange yu fazhan yanjiu)*. Beijing: China Agriculture Publishing House (Zhongguo nongye chuban she), 1998

Though measurement defects are inevitable, these deviations can have a serious impact on research outcomes. Therefore, it is necessary to understand the reasons behind the controversy and unreliability of statistics. For China, the origin of official statistical problems can be understood from two aspects: the transformation of official statistical systems and the political factors influencing these statistics.

- **The Official Statistical Systems:** Throughout the Mao era, China adopted the Soviet-style Material Product System[66] as the core of its national accounts, emphasising input and output data in physical terms. As all means of production were tightly controlled and operated by the government, the national statistical system was relatively straightforward in recoding and reporting economic activities, which facilitated central planners in setting production goals and distributing resources and welfare accordingly. This system differs greatly from the internationally agreed-upon System of National Accounts.[67]

[66] For detailed differences between the Material Product System and the System of National Accounts, please refer to Department for Economic and Social Information and Policy Analysis of the United Nations Statistics Division. *Use of the System of National Accounts in Economies in Transition*. New York: United Nations, 1996.

[67] See United Nations Statistics Division. "The System of National Accounts (SNA)." Https://unstats.un.org/unsd/nationalaccount/sna.asp. Accessed July 15, 2024.

The surge in private business and investment at the beginning of the Dengist reforms made China's economic system more complex than the original statistical system had been designed to handle. In this context, China's statistical system began its transformation. Only by the 1990s did China abandon the Material Product System and fully incorporated the international standard of the value-added approach to GDP. Meanwhile, a central-local two-tier statistical system was established to facilitate the transition to the conventional System of National Accounts. Hence, China's statistical system had long been systematically out of sync with international practices. This technical factor contributes to the lack of accuracy and reliability in China's statistics for academic use.

- **Political Factors Influencing Statistics:** The political movements during the Mao era rendered China's statistical data unreliable. For example, as mentioned earlier in this chapter, agricultural yield data during the "launching satellite" campaign was exaggerated to extreme levels that remain unmatched by today's technology. Another example is China's reported industrial contribution to GDP, which was officially stated as high as 47.7% in the 1970s, whereas the actual average share was around 20–30% after adjusting for scissor pricing distortions. Due to the influence of political movements, both industrial and agricultural data were systematically distorted, causing China's economic data to lack basic credibility throughout the entire Mao era.

  When the Dengist reforms ended China's prolonged political movements and prioritised economic growth, GDP became a crucial criterion in the "tournament"[68] model of cadre evaluation. In this context, GDP in reforming China was not only a statistic but also a measure of local officials' political achievements and governance capabilities. Under the newly established two-tier central-local statistical system, inflated local GDP figures became common as local officials sought to enhance their career prospects. This is why some critics of official data point to falsification at provincial and municipal

[68] Zhou, Li An. "The Incentive and Cooperation of Government Officials in the Political Tournaments: An Interpretation of the Prolonged Local Protectionism and Duplicative Investments in China (Jinsheng boyi zhong zhengfu guanyuan de jili yu hezuo: jianlun woguo difang baohu zhuyi he chongfu jianshe wenti changqi cunzai de yuanyin)." *Economic Research Journal (Jingji yanjiu)* 6 (2004): 33–40.

levels, claiming they are the main source of unreliable statistics in China.

Nevertheless, the importance of data "availability" sometimes outweighs "reliability." Despite these problems, the National Bureau of Statistics' official data remains the only complete and systematic dataset available, thus serving as the primary source for Chinese economic research to date.

The statistics used in this work are also based on official data released by the Ministry of Agriculture and the National Bureau of Statistics. There are two main considerations: first, only official data covers China's long-term rural changes, making cross-temporal comparisons of food-related issues possible in this work; second, although much of the data is biased, it is consistently biased within the same statistical system. Therefore, to minimise such biases, shares and year-on-year growth rates are employed as indictors of trends rather than being regarded as infallible in accuracy.

Additionally, this work also compares China's official data with other sources, such as the Food and Agriculture Organization of the United Nations and the United States Department of Agriculture, to provide a retrospective summary of key issues in China's agriculture and food security. When data problems arise, it is important to determine whether they stem from the statistical system and techniques, political factors, or a combination of both. If the available data indeed exhibits serious quality defects, appropriate adjustments are necessary to make research outcomes as unbiased as possible. Thus, the quality of China's official statistics has been carefully considered in this work.

Structure of the Work

Following an introduction to the food sector during Chinese industrialisation in Mao's era, the discussion will pivot to the evolution of agricultural development in transitioning China. It will also examine the reforming government's attitude towards the changing patterns of food issues in China.

Chapter 2 links food issues with socio-economic conditions, such as domestic food affordability, food access and inflation driven by consumption prices. Before the liberalisation of the food sector in 2003–2008, China's food sector pursued two primary objectives: firstly, ensuring sufficient staple food for its population; and secondly, transferring rural surpluses to the urban sector to support low-cost industrialisation. These objectives had dominated China's food policies until the 2000s, when rising residential incomes enabled the country to address long-standing food concerns against the backdrop of industrialisation. However, while increased income levels alleviated issues of grain supply and consumption inadequacy, a new challenge emerged: insufficient arable land. The demand for fodder grain far exceeded the food sector's maximum supply capacity due to limited arable resources.

Chapter 3 explores China's dependence on food imports, focussing on fodder grain imports before and after the onset of the Sino-US economic conflict. Following the announcement of tariffs on Chinese imports by the United States, China retaliated by imposing a significant 179% tariff on American sorghum. Additional levies were also applied to dried distillers' grains with solubles (DDGS), fish-bone power and fish meals. While considerable attention was given to the impact on American farmers, China's livestock industry faced serious repercussions due to its substantial reliance on imports of American fodder-based agricultural products. To this day, the United States remains the most crucial fodder exporter to China. In an effort to lessen its dependence on the United States, China is expected to adjust its fodder commodity imports, balancing between protein varieties and energy forage crops.

Chapter 4 hence delves into the evolving challenges to China's food issues. The first challenge concerns the persistent issue of hunger, which predominantly affects rural populations. The second challenge is China's dietary transition that began in the 2000s, shifting from a semi-vegetarian diet to one richer in animal proteins. This shift has heightened the demand for fodder grains, potentially prompting more imports. As China's labour supply has passed its peak and the population has started to decline, resource scarcity has become a significant constraint on meeting domestic grain needs. In this context, China's recently cultivated land totals 127.9 million hectares just exceeding the 1.8-billion-mu "red line" for basic food needs. This constraint underscores the scarcity of China's natural resources and complicates the achievement of food security across all economic sectors.

Chapter 5 examines the future prospects of China's food insecurity in light of changes in the international market environment and domestic rural income issues. As China has increased its participation in the international food market to supplement its food security, the global market has maintained a precarious balance, with little competition from other developing countries undergoing dietary transitions. However, over the past decade, several countries have reached the upper-middle-income bracket, experiencing rapid dietary shifts similar to those China faced in the 2000s and 2010s. As these latecomers gain significance in the international food market, potential supply and demand imbalances could pose risks to global food security, including China's, if agricultural technology remains unchanged in the near future. Meanwhile, when rural welfare has not been a concern in maintaining farmers' incentives for food self-sufficiency after the Chinese government supplementing the nation's food supply through overseas imports, the income gap within China's rural-urban divide has persisted. Additionally, food prices continue to be influenced by state-owned grain enterprises (*hereafter referred to as* grain SOEs). As a result, rural per capita income—whether derived from grain production or non-farming activities—remains significantly lower than urban per capita income. A side effect of the post-1979 economic miracle has been the growing disparity in income between rural and urban China. This chapter concludes with a retrospective summary of the key issues in China's agricultural track record and food security discussed in this work.

References

Allen, Robert C. *Global Economic History: A Very Short Introduction.* Oxford: Oxford University Press, 2011.

Allen, Robert C., Jean-Pascal Bassino, Debin Ma, Christine Moll-Murata, and Jan Luiten van Zanden. "Wages, Prices, and Living Standards in China, 1739–1925: In Comparison with Europe, Japan, and India." *Economic History Review* 64 (2011): 8–38.

Ash, Robert F. "Squeezing the Peasants: Grain Extraction, Food Consumption and Rural Living Standards in Mao's China." *The China Quarterly* 188 (2006): 959–998.

Ash, Robert F., Jane Du, and Cheng King. "Perspectives on Agricultural and Grain Output Growth in China from the Nineteenth Century to the Present Day." In Pinilla, V. and H. Willebald (eds.). *Agricultural Development in the World Periphery: A Global Economic History Approach.* London: Palgrave Macmillan, 2018.

Barnett, Arthur Doak. *China's Economy in Global Perspective.* Washington: Brookings Institution, 1981.

Becker, Jasper. *Hungry Ghosts: China's Secret Famine.* London: John Murray, 1996.

Bo, Yibo. *Recollections on Certain Major Policies and Events (Ruogan zhong da juece yu shijian de huigu)*, 2 volumes. Beijing: Central Party School Press (Zhonggong zhongyang dangxiao chubanshe), 1991.

Cao, Shuji. "The Deaths of China's Population and Its Root Cause during 1959–1961 (1959–1961 nian Zhongguo de renkou siwang ji qi chengyin)." *Chinese Journal of Population Science (Zhongguo renkou kexue)* 1 (2005): 14–28.

Central Committee of the CCP. *Resolution of the Central Committee of the Communist Party of China on Mutual Assistance and Collectivisation in Agricultural Production (Draft) (Zhonggong zhongyang guanyu nongye shengchan huzhu hezuo de jueyi [cao an])*. Beijing: Central Committee of the CCP, December 15, 1951.

Central Committee of the Chinese Communist Party. *Circular of the Central Committee on the "Report on the National Agricultural Work Conference" Issued by the Party Leadership Group of the Ministry of Agriculture (Zhonggong zhongyang zhuanfa nongye bu dangzu "guanyu quanguo nongye gongzuo huiyi de baogao")*. Beijing: Chinese Communist Party Central Committee, March 19, 1960.

Chinese People's Political Consultative Conference. *Common Programme of the Chinese People's Political Consultative Conference (Zhongguo renmin zhengzhi xieshang huiyi gongtong gangling)*. Beijing: Chinese People's Political Consultative, September 29, 1949.

Contemporary Agricultural History Research Office, Rural Economic Research Centre, Ministry of Agriculture (eds.) *A Study of Agricultural Reforms and Development in Contemporary China (Dangdai Zhongguo Nongye Biange Yu Fazhan Yanjiu)*. Beijing: China Agriculture Publishing House (Zhongguo Nongye Chuban She), 1998.

Deng, Keng, Jim H. Shen, and Jingyuan Guo. "Performance and Mechanisms of the Maoist Economy—A Holistic Approach, 1950–1980". *Journal of the Economic and Social History of the Orient* (2024): forthcoming. Http://eprints.lse.ac.uk/124262. Accessed August 30, 2024.

Department for Economic and Social Information and Policy Analysis of the United Nations Statistics Division. *Use of the System of National Accounts in Economies in Transition*. New York: United Nations, 1996.

Department of Price of the National Development and Reform Commission of China. *National Agricultural Costs and Returns Compilation*. Beijing: China Statistics Press, 2000–2023 editions.

Dikötter, Frank. *Mao's Great Famine: The History of Chinas Most Devastating Catastrophe, 1958–1962*. London: Bloomsbury, 2010.

Du, Jun. *Agricultural Transition in China: Domestic and International Perspectives on Technology and Institutional Change*. Basingstoke: Palgrave Macmillan, 2018.

Government Administrative Council of the Central People's Government of China. *Decree on Planned Procurement and Planned Supply of Food Grain*

(Guanyu shixing liangshi de jihua shougou he jihua gongying de mingling). Beijing: Government Administration Council of the Central People's Government of China, November 19, 1953.

Information Office of the State Council of China. *Food Security in China (Zhongguo de liangshi Anquan)*. Government White Paper. Published October 2019. Http://www.scio.gov.cn/ztk/dtzt/39912/41906/index.htm. Accessed January 15, 2024a.

Information Office of the State Council of China. *Grain Issues in China (Zhongguo de liangshi wenti)*. Government White Paper. Published in October 1996. Https://www.gov.cn/zhengce/2005-05/25/content_2615740.htm. Accessed January 15, 2024b.

Ishikawa, Shigeru. "Resource Flow between Agriculture and Industry—The Chinese Experience." *The Developing Economies* 5 (1967): 3–49.

Kuo, Leslie Tse-Chiu. *The Technical Transformation of Agriculture in Communist China*. New York: Praeger Press, 1972.

Lardy, Nicholas R. *Agriculture in China's Modern Economic Development*. Cambridge: Cambridge University Press, 1983.

Lee, Frank C. "Land Redistribution in Communist China." *Pacific Affairs* 21 (1948): 20–32.

Lin, Justin Y. "Collectivization and China's Agricultural Crisis in 1959–1961." *Journal of Political Economy* 98 (1990): 1228–1252.

Lin, Justin Y. "Inflation and Growth in China's Transition: A Comparison with Eastern Europe and the Former Soviet Union." In Guitian, Manuel, and Robert A. Mundell (eds.). *Inflation and Growth in China: Proceedings of a Conference Held in Beijing, China May 10-12, 1995*. Washington: International Monetary Fund, 1996. Https://www.elibrary.imf.org/display/book/9781557755421/ch015.xml. Accessed January 15, 2024.

Lyons, Thomas P. "Feeding Fujian: Grain Production and Trade, 1986–1996." *The China Quarterly* 155 (1998): 512–545.

Mao, Zedong. *Collected Works of Mao Zedong*, Volume 6. Beijing: People's Publishing House (Renmin chuban she), 1951 [1992].

Mao, Zedong. *Mao Zedong's Manuscripts Since the Founding of the State (Jianguo yilai Mao Zedong wengao)*, volume 7. Beijing: Central Literature Publishing House (Zhongyang wenxian chuban she), 1958 [1992].

Mao, Zedong. *Selected Works of Mao Tse-Tung*, Volume V. Beijing: People's Publishing House (Renmin chuban she), 1977 [2014].

National Bureau of Statistics of China. *China Statistical Yearbook (Zhongguo tongji nianjian)*. Beijing: China Statistics Press (Zhongguo tongji chuban she), 1981–2023 editions.

National Bureau of Statistics of China. National Data. Https://data.stats.gov.cn/english/easyquery.htm. Accessed January 15, 2024.

Office of Agricultural Statistics, National Bureau of Statistics of China. *Brilliant Accomplishments of China's Agriculture 1949–1984* (*Zhongguo nongye de guanghui chengjiu 1949–1984*). Beijing: China Statistics Press (Zhongguo tongji chuban she), 1984.

Peng, Xizhe. "Demogrpahic Consequences of the Great Leap Forward in China's Provinces." *Population and Development Review* 13 (1987): 639–670.

Perkins, Dwight H. (ed.). *China's Modern Economy in Historical Perspective.* Stanford: Stanford University Press, 1975.

Qian, Xuesen. "How Much Grain Yield per Mu? (Liangshi muchan liang huiyou duoshao)." *China Youth Daily (Zhongguo qingnian bao),* published on 16 June 1958.

Ryan, James. *Lenin's Terror, the Ideological Origin of Early Soviet State Violence.* London: Routledge, 2012.

Sun, Jian. *Economic History of China: Modern Section, 1840–1949 (Zhongguo jingji shi: jindai bufen, 1840–1949 nian).* Beijing: China Renmin University Press (Zhongguo renmin daxue chuban she), 1989.

Tian, Xiquan. "The Grain Crisis, the General Line for the Transitional Period and the Promulgation of the Policy for Unified Purchase and Sale of Grain (1953 nian liangshi weiji yu tonggou tongxiao zhengce de chutai)." *Journal of East China Normal University (Philosophy and Social Sciences) (Huadong shifan daxue xuebao [zhexue shehui kexue ban])* 39 (2007): 54–60.

United Nations Statistics Division. "The System of National Accounts (SNA)." Https://unstats.un.org/unsd/nationalaccount/sna.asp. Accessed July 15, 2024.

United States Department of Agriculture. National Agricultural Statistics Services. Http://www.nass.usda.gov. Accessed January 15, 2024.

Vermeer, Eduard B. *Water Conservancy and Irrigation in China: Social, Economic and Agrotechnical Aspects.* Leiden: Leiden University Press, 1977.

Walker, Kenneth R. "Collectivisation in Retrospect: The 'Socialist High Tide' of Autumn 1955–Spring 1956." *The China Quarterly* 26 (1966): 1–43.

Walker, Kenneth R. "Organization for Agricultural Production." In Eckstein, Alexander, Walter Galenson, and Ta-Chung Liu (eds.). *Economic Trends in Communist China.* Edinburgh: Edinburgh University Press, 1968.

Wu, Chengming. Modernization in China: *Market and Society (Zhongguo de xiandaihua: shichang uu shehui).* Beijing: SDX Joint Publishing Company, 2001.

Wu, Li. "Dialectic Discussion on the Price Gap in China's 'Price Scissors' from 1949 to 1978 (1949–1978 nian zhongguo 'jian dao cha' cha'e bianzheng)." *Researches in Chinese Economic History (Zhongguo jingji shi yanjiu)* 4 (2001): 3–12.

Yang, Jisheng. "A Historical Review of the State Monopoly over Procurement and Retailing (Tonggou tongxiao de lishi huigu)." *Yanhuang Chunqiu* 12 (2008): 48–54.

Yang, Jisheng. *Tombstone: The Untold Story of Mao's Great Famine*. London: Allen Lane, 2012.

Zhou, Li An. "The Incentive and Cooperation of Government Officials in the Political Tournaments: An Interpretation of the Prolonged Local Protectionism and Duplicative Investments in China (Jinsheng boyi zhong zhengfu guanyuan de jili yu hezuo: jianlun woguo difang baohu zhuyi he chongfu jianshe wenti changqi cunzai de yuanyin)." *Economic Research Journal (Jingji yanjiu)* 6 (2004): 33–40.

Zweig, David. *Agrarian Radicalism in China, 1968–1981*. Cambridge, Massachusetts, and London: Harvard University Press, 1989.

CHAPTER 2

Food Sector in the Dual-Track System Under the Dengist Reforms

Abstract This chapter explores the link between food issues and socio-economic conditions, such as domestic food affordability, food access and inflation driven by consumption prices. Before the liberalisation of the food sector between 2003 and 2008, China's food sector operated with two primary objectives. First, it aimed to ensure the provision of sufficient staple food for the Chinese population. Secondly, it endeavoured to transfer rural surplus to the urban sector, thereby supporting low-cost industrialisation. These objectives remained central to China's food policies until the 2000s, when improvements in residential incomes enabled the country to tackle long-standing food-related concerns amidst ongoing industrialisation. However, as rising income levels addressed issues of grain supply and consumption inadequacies, a new challenge emerged. The scarcity of arable land led to the demand for fodder grain significantly outstripping the food sector's maximum supply capacity in China.

Keywords De-collectivisation • Economic opening • Dengist (agricultural) reforms • Total factor productivity • Food output • Food accessibility • Food availability • Food affordability • The Grain Bureau • Inflation • Marketisation

J. Du, *Farmland, Farming and Food in the National Economy of China, 1947–2020*, Palgrave Studies in Economic History,
https://doi.org/10.1007/978-3-031-70027-9_2

The Dengist Reforms in Agriculture

Food deficits and stagnant per capita output have signalled low agricultural efficiency[1] in China. A substantial portion of rural surplus was transferred to the industrial sector through the centrally planned food system, with the aim of accelerating rapid industrialisation.[2] However, this approach resulted in severe distortions within the agricultural sector[3] and impeded output growth.

The Dengist reforms began with de-collectivisation of agriculture through the implementation of the Household Responsibility System (*jiating lianchan chengbao zerenzhi*), which reinstated household-based production in rural China. This reform is widely acknowledged by scholars as a pivotal driver of agricultural development during the 1980s.[4] With

[1] According to the United States Department of Agriculture's *International Agricultural Productivity* data, the total factor productivity (TFP) indices of agriculture in China during the 1960s and 1970s fluctuated between 34 and 38 (with 2015 as the base year, set at 100). The lowest productivity was recorded in 1977, right after the Culture Revolution. This implies that, throughout the 1960s and 1970s, China's agricultural TFP was only about one-third of what it has been in recent years. For more detailed productivity data, refer to the United States Department of Agriculture. *International Agricultural Total Factor Productivity Indices, 1961–2021.* Https://www.ers.usda.gov/data-products/international-agricultural-productivity. Accessed January 15, 2024.

[2] The Chinese state maintained stringent control over the entire food sector through the manipulation of food procurement and retail prices. This system of price manipulation was employed to divert agricultural surplus towards industrial development. The deliberately suppressed prices of food helped maintain low wage levels for Chinese labour, thereby supporting China's industrialisation by providing a cost advantage through reduced labour costs. For further reading on this topic, refer to the works of Du, Jane, and Cheng King. "Unravelling China's Food Security Puzzle, 1979–2008." *The China Quarterly* 235 (2018): 804–827; and Du, Jane, and Kent Deng. "Getting Food Prices Right: The State versus the Market in Reforming China, 1979–2006." *European Review of Economic History* 21(2017): 302–325.

[3] For a detailed analysis of the negative effects of rural-to-urban welfare transfers on China's agricultural sector, interested readers should consult the following sources: Fan, Qimiao, and Peter Nolan (eds.). *China's Economic Reforms: The Costs and Benefits of Incrementalism.* Basingstoke: Palgrave Macmillan, 1994; Lardy, Nicholas R. *Agriculture in China's Modern Economic Development.* Cambridge: Cambridge University Press, 1983; Lin, Justin Y. "An Economic Theory of Institutional Change: Induced and Imposed Change." *Cato Journal* 9 (1989): 1–33.

[4] For studies on the early years of post-1979 agricultural reforms (e.g. Household Responsibility System), please refer to the following sources: Lin, Justin Y. "The Household Responsibility System Reform and the Adoption of Hybrid Rice in China." *Journal of Development Economics* 36 (1991): 353–372; and McMillan, John, John Whalley, and Lijing Zhu. "The Impact of China's Economic Reforms on Agricultural Productivity Growth." *Journal of Political Economy* 97 (1989): 781–807.

re-establishment of the agricultural produce market in 1979, Chinese farmers regained price sensitivity and rapidly adjusted to increased procurement prices. Collectively, these changes led to a swift increase in grain output following the reforms.

To better understand the enduring priorities related to food under the Dengist government, the analysis uses grain (i.e. rice) output and its procurement prices as proxies, tracing developments back to 1979. This period marked the first instance since the Great Leap Famine when the Chinese state explicitly emphasised its commitment to food security.

As depicted in Fig. 2.1, the Dengist reforms in the food sector can be chronologically divided into four distinct phases.[5]

- The first phase, from 1979 to 1985, was characterised by a rapid increase in food output, which was followed by a period of fluctuation beginning in 1985.
- The second phase, from 1986 to 1993, saw the Chinese government undertakes extensive reforms in its food circulation system, culminating in the complete abolition of the urban ration food coupon system.

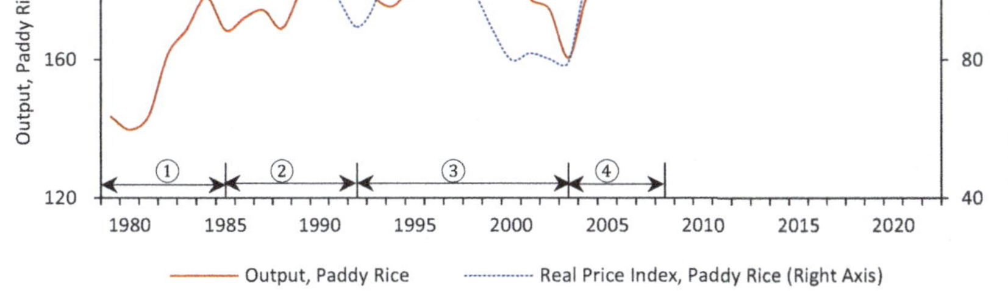

Fig. 2.1 Rice production and price changes since the Dengist reforms

[5] For details, refer to Du, Jane, and Cheng King. "Unravelling China's Food Security Puzzle, 1979–2008." *The China Quarterly* 235 (2018): 804–827.

- The third phase, starting in 1993, was marked by the grain reforms that drove grain output to a historical peak. However, this peak was followed by a rapid decline that ended in 2003.
- The fourth phase, from 2003 to 2008, saw the state-implemented policies to ease grain market constraints, stimulating a revival of the domestic food supply.

The output of major grain crops during these phases is detailed in Table 2.1.

Reforming Institutions in the Food Sector

De-collectivisation in the Early 1980s

After the Great Leap Famine and Cultural Revolution (*wenhua da geming*), the collectivisation of agricultural production in China faced a number of challenges, the most severe of which was food shortage. Rural Chinese communities were kept at a mere subsistence level. In 1978, households in Xiaogang Village, Anhui province, singed a secret agreement in which collectively owned farmland was divided into household plots, with each household responsible for its own losses and profits from farming. This marked the beginning of the transformation of food production back to a household-based model.

From the beginning of the Dengist reforms, there was a shift towards prioritising food production. The initial phase of these reforms was characterised by the de-collectivisation of agriculture, facilitated by the introduction of the Household Responsibility System, which was developed from the trial conducted in Xiaogang Village.

This system, combined with higher-than-market grain procurement prices in 1984 (Fig. 2.1) for both state quota and above-quota grain, meant that fulfilling the state's grain quota was no longer viewed as an agricultural tax. The Household Responsibility System, along with the comprehensive increase in grain purchase prices, stabilised peasant's expectations regarding farming income, leading to remarkable improvements in China's food production. Specifically, there were successive harvests that saw a significant increase in output: rice production rose by 24.0% and wheat production by 40.0% compared to levels in 1979[6] (Table 2.1).

[6]Rice production experienced a significant surge, increasing from 143.8 million tonnes in 1979 to 178.3 million tonnes, while wheat production rose from 62.7 million tonnes to 82.7 million tonnes.

Table 2.1 Food output under the Dengist reforms

	Grain output (million tonnes)				
	Grain, total	*Rice, paddy*	*Wheat*	*Maize*	*Soybean*
	(1)	(2)	(3)	(4)	(5)
Phase 1					
1979	332.1	143.8	62.7	60.0	7.5
1980	320.6	139.9	55.2	62.6	7.9
1981	325.0	144.0	59.6	59.2	9.3
1982	354.5	161.6	68.5	60.6	9.0
1983	387.3	168.9	81.4	68.2	9.8
1984	407.3	178.3	87.8	73.4	9.7
Phase 2					
1985	379.1	168.6	85.8	63.8	10.5
1986	391.5	172.2	90.0	70.9	11.6
1987	404.7	174.4	87.8	79.8	12.2
1988	394.1	169.1	85.4	77.4	11.6
1989	407.5	180.1	90.8	78.9	10.2
1990	446.2	189.3	98.2	96.8	11.0
1991	435.3	183.8	96.0	98.8	9.7
1992	442.7	186.2	101.6	95.4	10.3
1993	456.5	177.5	106.4	102.7	15.3
Phase 3					
1994	445.1	175.9	99.3	99.3	16.0
1995	466.6	185.2	102.2	112.0	13.5
1996	504.5	195.1	110.6	127.5	13.2
1997	494.2	200.7	123.3	104.3	14.7
1998	512.3	198.7	109.7	133.0	15.2
1999	508.4	198.5	113.9	128.1	14.2
2000	462.2	187.9	99.6	106.0	15.4
2001	452.6	177.6	93.9	114.1	15.4
2002	457.1	174.5	90.3	121.3	16.5
2003	430.7	160.7	86.5	115.8	15.4
Phase 4					
2004	469.5	179.1	92.0	130.3	17.4
2005	484.0	180.6	97.4	139.4	16.3
2006	498.0	181.7	108.5	151.6	15.1
2007	504.1	186.4	109.5	155.1	12.8
2008	534.3	192.6	112.9	172.1	15.7

Source: National Bureau of Statistics of China. *China Statistical Yearbook (Zhongguo tongji nianjian)*. Beijing: China Statistics Press (Zhongguo tongji chuban she), 1981–2023 editions; National Bureau of Statistics of China. National Data. Https://data.stats.gov.cn/english/easyquery.htm. Accessed January 15, 2024

The substantial expansion of grain output, coupled with a rapid increase in grain prices, introduced a new challenge: a significant fiscal burden on the Chinese government. Document no. 137 from 1982[7] highlighted this concern, noting "the rapid increase in food grain circulation has surpassed the government's financial capacity."[8] To alleviate this fiscal pressure, several options were considered, the most direct of which included reducing the quantity of grain purchases or decreasing the grain purchase price. Opting to reduce the quantity of grain purchases could have immediately jeopardised grain supply, compelling the Dengist government to choose instead to lower the purchase price.

In 1985, a new pricing rule termed the "reverse 30:70 ratio" (*dao san qi*)[9] was enacted. According to the "reverse 30:70 ratio," the grain procurement price was determined by a formula: 30% of the price was based on the food grain quota, while the remaining 70% was derived from the price of grain sold above the quota.

On the surface, the "reverse 30:70 ratio" appeared to offer farmers a higher "quota" price as specified in their "contracts." However, in practice, this policy did not result in an increase in marginal income for the farmers. This discrepancy arose because the price for grain sold "above the quota" was adjusted downwards to match the quota price of the preceding year under this new rule. Consequently, the actual procurement price for rice declined by 6.9% in 1986 compared to its level in 1984, while the purchase price for wheat declined by 10.3%.

[7] State Council of China. "Document No. 137 of 1982. *Circular on the Diligent Execution of All Operations Affecting Grain (Guowuyuan guanyu renzhen zuohao liangshi gongzuo de tongzhi)*." Beijing: State Council of China, November 28, 1982.

[8] Ibid.

[9] In the specified year, the above-quota price was set at 1.5 times the previous year's quota price. According to the "reversed 30:70 ratio," the contracted grain procurement price was then approximately 1.4 times higher than the quota price from the year before. However, Central Committee Document No. 1 of 1985 introduced a policy in which the government committed to purchasing food grain that exceeded contract levels at the assured price (*bao hu jia*), which was equivalent to the quota price from the year before. This adjustment resulted in the procurement price for above-contract food grain in 1985 reverting to the 1984 quota price. In practice, this "reversed 30:70 ratio" policy negatively affected farmer's incentives by reducing their marginal revenue by 50%. For more details, refer to the Central Committee of the CCP's "*Document No.1. 1985. Ten Policies of the Central Committee and the State Council for Further Enlivening the Rural Economy (Zhonggong zhongyang guowuyuan guanyu jinyibu huoyue nongcun jingji de shixiang zhengce)*." Beijing: CCP Central Committee, January 1, 1985.

Within just six years of the reform, the grain procurement pricing system underwent two substantial policy adjustments: the 1979 rapid rise in the state procurement price and the 1985 implementation of the "reverse 30:70 ratio." All these changes in the procurement prices during the recovery period led to fluctuations in farmers' incentives to produce. This instability is widely regarded as the main catalyst for the subsequent contraction in agricultural production, culminating in a prolonged period of output deceleration that lasted until 1989—a phase often referred to as the post-1985 slowdown.

Two-Sided Effects of Inflation since the Late 1980s

Starting in the mid-1980s, the deregulation of the industrial pricing system resulted in a substantial increase in the prices of manufactured goods. This encompassed essential agricultural inputs and a majority of goods consumed in rural areas. Despite this, the pricing of grain within the agricultural sector remained under strict control. In other words, during the 1986–1993 reforms, rural income continued to depend on the price-regulated market for agricultural products, while expenses were incurred from purchasing unregulated manufactured industrial products. Concurrently, inflation, which prevailed from the late 1980s (specifically from 1987 to 1993), caused a substantial increase in the prices of all industrial products, including most farming inputs (Fig. 2.2). Consequently, the purchasing power of those within the food sector declined.

To ensure a consistent grain supply amid high inflation, the government implemented a set of price policies designed to incentivise farming. Thanks to these stimulus measures and increases in procurement price, grain output began to rebound towards the end of the 1980s. By 1990, both rice and wheat outputs had achieved their historical peak levels since 1949 (Table 2.1).[10]

[10] In 1990, rice output in China reached a milestone of 189.3 million tonnes, surpassing the previous peak in 1984 by 11.1 million tonnes. This represented an increase of 31.7% from the production levels recorded in 1979. Furthermore, wheat output in 1990 soared to 98.2 million tonnes, marking a substantial growth of 56.6% since the post-1979 reform.

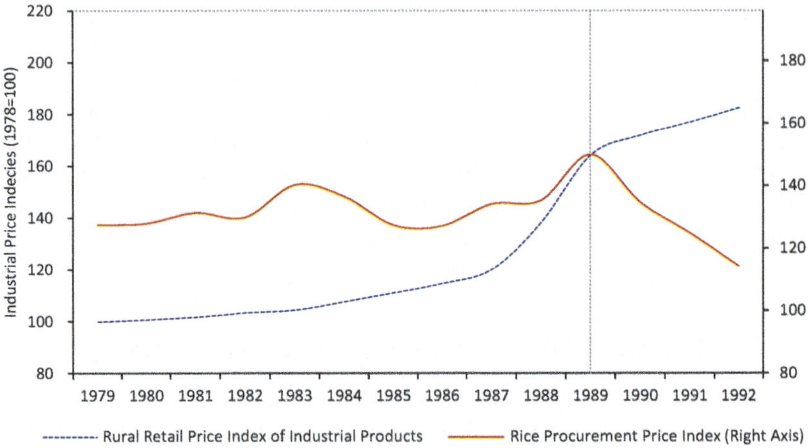

Fig. 2.2 Price indices for input and output products in rural China, 1979–1992

Nevertheless, the grain harvest of 1989–1990 had its own particularities. Amid rapidly growing inflationary pressures from 1987 to 1989, much of the nominal increase in grain procurement prices was offset. The real grain purchase price remained almost unchanged (see Fig. 2.2), while inflation significantly drove up the cost of food grain production. The ever-decreasing returns from grain production eventually dissuaded many farmers from "signing" procurement contracts with the state.[11] In response, the Chinese State Council terminated contractual procurement in 1990, opting instead for fixed procurement quotas through a policy known as "compulsory state procurement" (*guojia dinggou*).[12]

[11] The substantial decrease in the real grain purchase price also resulted in a quick and significant short-term decline in grain production. Between 1990 and 1993, paddy rice production dropped from 189.3 million tonnes to 177.5 million tonnes, with a further reduction to 175.9 million tonnes in 1994. Detailed data can be found in Table 2.1.

[12] Contractual procurement was more negotiable in nature compared to the compulsory state procurement policies.

Recovering from a slowdown in grain output that had persisted since 1985, China's grain production experienced a resurgence from the late 1980s. This resurgence necessitated a substantial allocation from the state budget for the procurement and distribution of grain. Alongside an expanding grain purchase budget due to consecutive bumper harvests, the Chinese government relinquished its pricing rights over urban grain distribution. A new pricing policy, "procurement and sales at the same price" (*gouxiao tongjia*), was instituted.[13] The grain circulation reform of 1992 marked a pivotal shift in the grain pricing system. These policies indicated that fiscal constraints compelled the central government to relinquish control over grain pricing and significantly reduce its direct urban subsidies in subsequent reforms.

The Decline of the Grain Bureau in 1993–2003

After Deng Xiaoping's southern inspection tour (*nan xun*), a new wave of reforms was initiated. In 1993,[14] the Chinese government made the decision to "liberalise food grain pricing and sales over the next two to three years" and to completely abolish the urban ration food coupon system within the following three years. This decision set the stage for anticipated comprehensive marketisation reforms of the nationwide food circulation system. However, by the mid-1990s, persistent inflation caused a sharp rise in the nominal selling price of urban grain in 1993 and 1994.[15] To ensure a stable food supply and maintain social stability, the state reasserted control over all grain-related work (*liangshi gongzuo*) in 1994, distancing them from market forces. Consequently, the marketisation of grain circulation, which had begun only several months earlier as part of the 1993 reforms, was reversed.

[13] For details, refer to the State Council of China. "*Document No.15 of 1992. Decisions of the State Council on Increasing the State Monopoly Selling Price of Grain (Guowuyuan guanyu tigao liangshi tongxiao jiage de jueding).*" Beijing: State Council of China, March 6, 1992.

[14] State Council of China. "*Document No. 9 of 1993. Circular of the State Council on Speeding up Reform of the Grain Circulation System (Guowuyuan guanyu jiakuai liangshi liutong tizhi gaige de tongzhi).*" Beijing: State Council of China, February 15, 1993.

[15] Compared to the preceding year, China's consumer price indices (CPI) increased by 14.7% in 1993 and by 24.1% in 1994.

In 1994, the issuance of State Council Document No. 32[16] and General Office of the State Council Document No. 76[17] transferred all grain trading activities from market operations back to governmental control, specifically to the Grain Bureau (*liangshi ju*) and its affiliated grain SOEs. Alongside this reassertion of control over grain circulation in 1994, the government also raised the grain purchase price in 1995–1996.[18] Subsequently, during the years 1995–1997, total grain output surged to the highest level ever recorded in the history of the PRC.[19] However, the increase in the grain procurement price, combined with the strengthened grain circulation system, not only led to abundant harvests but also resulted in an exceptionally large fiscal deficit. This situation compelled the Chinese government to enhance oversight over grain purchase funds (*liangshi shougou zijin*) and the Grain Bureau.

In early 1996, the government tightened its grain budget and mandated that all grain purchase funds be subject to joint monitoring by the Agricultural Development Bank of China (*Zhongguo nongye yinhang*) and the State Ministry of Finance. Despite these efforts, this initiative did not achieve its intended goal of curbing government expenditures on grain procurement. Under this collaborative monitoring system, the grain system's size expanded, and operational costs escalated.[20] By 1998, State Council Document No. 15[21] starkly announced that "the central

[16] State Council of China. "*Document No. 32 of 1994. Circular of the State Council on the Further Reform of Grain Purchase and Selling System (Guowuyuan guanyu shenhua liangshi gouxiao tizhi gaige de tongzhi).*" Beijing: State Council of China, May 9, 1994.

[17] General Office of the State Council of China. "*Documents No. 76 of 1994. Circular of the General Office of the State Council on Tightening up the Management of Grain Markets and Maintaining Stability of the Market (Guowuyuan bangongting guanyu jiaqiang liang shi shichang guanli baochi shichang wending de tongzhi).*" Beijing: General Office of the State Council of China, June 16, 1994.

[18] Compared to the nominal rice procurement price in 1992, the state increased the procurement price by 39.1% in 1995.

[19] In 1995, the output levels of rice and wheat were comparable to those recorded in 1990, with a modest increase observed in 1996. By 1997, however, both crops reached unprecedented heights since 1949. Rice production soared to 200.7 million tonnes, a 6.0% increase over its previous peak in 1990. Similarly, wheat production increased to 123.3 million tonnes, representing a 25.5% growth from the 1990 figures.

[20] This refers to the total number of employees and the extent of administration work across the entire state-owned grain procurement and circulation system.

[21] State Council of the China. "*Document No. 15 of 1998. Decision of the State Council on Further Reform over the Grain Circulation System (Guowuyuan guanyu jinyibu shenhua liangshi liutong tizhi gaige de jueding).*" Beijing: State Council of the China, May 10, 1998.

government's finances were now overwhelmed." The attempted reform efforts targeting the grain purchase fund had proven unsuccessful.

The failure of the 1996–1997 reform can be explained by the fact that the grain purchase fund essentially acted as a conduit for fiscal leakage. Simply regulating this channel did not tackle the root cause of the leakage—the Grain Bureau itself. Despite the 1994 overhaul, which reinforced grain-related work, the Grain Bureau continued to be perceived by the Chinese government as the most effective policy instrument for managing grain circulation. As a result, the reform efforts never moved beyond addressing the Grain Bureau as long as the central government's fiscal capacity was not critically constrained.[22] When it became clear that regulating the grain purchase fund was insufficient to alleviate the state's fiscal pressures, the policy emphasis shifted from merely regulating the use of grain purchase funds to reforming the underlying cause of fiscal leakage—the Grain Bureau itself.

Accordingly, the 1998 Grain Purchase Regulations[23] explicitly targeted the Grain Bureau system.[24] The primary focus of the 1998 Grain Purchase Regulations was to manage the deficits within the grain SOEs affiliated with the Grain Bureau. For the first time since the founding of the PRC, the state mandated that the Grain Bureau system adopt independent financial operations, acknowledging that the government's fiscal capacity could no longer sustain the system's deficits. Although the 1998 regulations succeeded in alleviating fiscal strain, they also transferred all pricing authority for grain procurement and sales to the grain SOEs through policies such as "pricing (grain) based on quality" (*anzhi lunjia*) and "selling (grain) at a favourable price" (*shunjia xiaoshou*). Moreover, the 1998 Grain Purchase Regulations defined the scope of trading for grain SOEs and established operational boundaries they were not allowed to exceed.

[22] For example, to alleviate fiscal pressures, the state terminated the long-standing urban grain subsidies in 1993. Despite this move, no significant policies or regulations were introduced to reform grain enterprises, resulting in continued fiscal leakages.

[23] State Council of the China. "*Decree No. 244 of 1998. Regulations on Grain Purchase (Liangshi shougou tiaoli).*" Beijing: State Council of China, June 6, 1998.

[24] The state implemented a new guiding rule for the management of the Grain Bureau in August 1997, termed "cost plus slim profit" (*baoben weili*). This rule granted grain SOEs the authority to "mark up the grain price" (*shunjia zuojia*) accordingly. The primary aim of this rule was to empower grain SOEs with the autonomy to manage their own profits and losses, effectively making them financially independent from central finance. Nevertheless, from the Grain Bureau's perspective, the urban selling price of food grain was permitted to yield a profit after covering the operational costs of the grain SOEs.

This restructuring led to the fragmentation of China's agricultural market into smaller, localised segments. In each segment, a local monopoliser—either a local Grain Bureau or a grain SOE—controlled all grain trade within that market.

The 1998 grain reform further tightened control over the food circulation system, marking a departure from the 1993 grain marketisation. While these reforms successfully prevented grain shortages, the outcome of was however a shift from a state grain monopoly to a unique monopoly on food grain circulation exercised by the Grain Bureau system. In practice, this change inadvertently empowered affiliated grain SOEs to collaborate with local governments, enabling them to suppress the farm gate price of grain procurement to maximise profits. Coupled with a reduction in the minimum grain protection price (*zuidi liangshi baohu jiage*), real rice and wheat procurement prices in 2000 plummeted to their bottom levels since 1979.[25]

Food Market Liberalisation in 2003–2008

Since 1998, there has been a consecutive decline in the production of rice and wheat, coinciding with a decrease in the real procurement price. By 2003, the output these staples had fallen to levels comparable to those in 1982 for rice and 1984 for wheat (Table 2.1).[26] This downturn posed a significant challenge to the Chinese government and resembled the most severe systemic grain crisis since the opening-up reforms. In response to the 2003 crisis, Beijing recognised the need to liberalise China's grain market. Furthermore, it aimed to reconstruct the state's subsidy

[25] The minimum grain protection price system was initially established in 1990 as a tool by the government to guide annual grain procurement pricing and protect farmers' interests. This system, alongside the national strategic grain reserve system, was designed to balance grain demand and supply, thereby stabilising grain market prices. However, following the 1998 reform, the authority to set grain prices, with the exception of the minimum grain protection price, was transferred from the Chinese government to grain SOEs. Facing escalating grain fiscal deficits, the central government revised the minimum grain protection price system in 1999, significantly impacting the prices at which grains were purchased from farmers. As a result, the real grain purchase price saw a sharp decline during the period of 1999–2000 (Fig. 2.1). Moreover, by 2003, the procurement price for wheat and rice (adjusted for CPI) had fallen to 64.1% and 80.1%, respectively, of their 1979 levels.

[26] In 2003, rice and wheat production levels fell to 80.0% and 70.2%, respectively, of their 1997 totals.

mechanism for grain producers, as outlined in the Central Committee of the CCP's Document No. 1 in 2004.[27]

In the subsequent Document No. 17[28] announced by the State Council, adjustments were made to the protection prices for major grain varieties. Additionally, the State Council initiated direct subsidise to grain farming households through county-level governments. This policy marked the first instance since 1949 of the government providing subsidies to agricultural producers. For nearly half a century, the Chinese state had relied on the surplus from rural food producers to finance industrialisation.

In pursuit of establishing a liberalised agricultural product market, as outlined in the Document No. 1 of 2004, the State Council in its Decree No. 407[29] explicitly stipulated that grain procurement and selling prices would be determined by the market. This action formally terminated the Grain Purchase Regulations implemented in 1998 and reaffirmed principles of the 1993 version of China's Agricultural Law.[30] The reforms of 2003–2004 were a continuation of the marketisation process initiated in 1993. While the 1993 reform involved a pilot test of utilising grain SOEs to maintain the state monopoly on grain, the systemic grain crisis of 2003

[27] Central Committee of the CCP. "*Document No. 1 of 2004b. Opinions of the Central Committee and the State Council Concerning Several Policies on Promoting the Increase of Farmers' (Income Zhonggong zhongyang, guowuyuan guanyu cujin nongmin zengjia shouru ruogan zhengce de yijian).*" Beijing: Central Committee of the CCP and the State Council of China, December 31, 2003.

[28] State Council of China. "*Document No. 17 of 2004a. Opinions of the State Council on Further Deepening the Reform to the Grain Distribution System (Guowuyuan guanyu jinyibu shenhua liangshi liutong tizhi gaige de yijian).*" Beijing: State Council of China, May 23, 2004.

[29] State Council of China. "*Decree No. 407 of 2004. Regulations on Administration of Grain Distribution (Liangshi liutong guanli tiaoli).*" Beijing: The State Council of China, May 26, 2004.

[30] The 1993 Agricultural Law (dated July 2, 1993) attempted to promote marketisation reform within China's agricultural sector. The Chinese government, for the first time, adopted legal measures to officially introduce a free market system for the distribution of agricultural products. However, the subsequent surge in grain price, driven by a high CPI and the failure of the breakthrough in the price liberalisation, compelled the central government to retract its involvement from the market in 1994. This reversal signalled the abandonment of the marketisation principles established in the 1993 version of China's Agricultural Law. For more information, refer to the Second Session of the Ninth Standing Committee of the National People's Congress of China. *Agriculture Law of the People's Republic of China (Zhonghua renmin gongheguo nongye fa)*. Beijing: National People's Congress, July 2, 1993.

compelled the Chinese state to decisively opt for the liberalisation of grain circulation, leaving all aspects of grain-related work to market forces.

After 2004, China's food policy reverted back to a market-oriented approach. The Central Committee of the CCP, through its Document No. 1 of 2005[31] and 2006,[32] emphasised the cancellation of the agricultural tax. In subsequent years, particular through Document No. 1[33] of 2007 and 2008, the Chinese government gradually increased subsidies for grain production and reinforced marketisation as the principal direction of the government's rural reform strategy.

By the end of 2008, the Chinese government reaffirmed its commitment to food security through the *Medium and Long-Term Plan for National Food Security (2008–2020)*.[34] Unlike the reforms of previous years, grain production after 2008 consistently maintained high levels (see Fig. 2.1). These years of abundant grain harvests effectively ensured national food security, primarily through the lens of staple food self-sufficiency. However, China experienced a new wave of high inflation since 2008. Unlike the period from 1988 to 1992, the increases in grain production costs during this later period were offset by a corresponding rise in the nominal grain retail price, a change determined by the market dynamics.

[31] Central Committee of the CCP. "*Document No. 1 of 2005. Opinions of the Central Committee and the State Council Concerning Several Policies on Further Strengthening Rural Works and Promoting the Comprehensive Agricultural Productivities (Zhonggong zhongyang, guowuyuan guanyu jin yibu jiaqiang nongcun gongzuo tigao nongye zonghe shengchan nengli ruogan zhengce de yijian).*" Beijing: Central Committee of the CCP and the State Council of China, December 31, 2004.

[32] Central Committee of the CCP. "*Document No. 1 of 2006. Opinions of the Central Committee and the State Council on Promoting the Construction of the New Socialist Country (Zhonggong zhongyang, guowuyuan guanyu tuijin shehui zhuyi xin nongcun jianshe de ruogan yijian).*" Beijing: Central Committee of the CCP and the State Council of China, December 31, 2005.

[33] Central Committee of the CCP. "*Document No. 1 of 2007. Opinions of the Central Committee and the State Council on Actively Developing Modern Agriculture and Steady Promoting the Construction of the New Socialist Country (Zhonggong zhongyang, guowuyuan guanyu jiji fazhan xiandai nongye zhashi tuijin shehui zuyi xin nongce jianshe de ruogan yijian).*" Beijing: Central Committee of the CCP and the State Council of China, December 31, 2006.

[34] National Development and Reform Commission of China. *Medium and Long-term Plan for National Food Security 2008–2020 (Guojia liangshi anquan zhongchangqi guihua gangyao 2008–2020 nian).* Beijing: National Development and Reform Committee, November 13, 2008.

Peasants in the Dual-Track System

The de-collectivisation effort in the 1980s largely restored production incentives among peasants.[35] In the agricultural reform of 1983,[36] farmland was reallocated to individual rural households. Although grain procurement prices remained under the control of the Grain Bureau, peasants' economic gains however became directly linked to their levels of grain output. Consequently, the monetary income from selling grain quickly enhanced the peasants' effort levels.

In addition to monetary gains from selling grain, rural households regained their planting decision rights after the reforms. While the Chinese government continued to enforce compulsory procurement quotas for farm produce, the procurement prices offered to rural households for these quotas were however much higher than before the reforms. This increase in procurement prices, combined with enhanced production incentives and the widespread adoption of Green Revolution technologies, led to a notable rise in per-hectare grain output. Since the 1983 reforms, grain plantation decision-making became less influenced by government-assigned production responsibilities; rather, it was more closely linked to peasants' economic considerations. As a result, the sown areas for wheat and rice began to decline, while the planting areas for soybeans and maize surged due to changes in relative prices.[37]

Despite the liberalising reforms of the opening-up policy, the Chinese government maintained tight control over grain circulation, specifically prohibiting non-state-owned enterprises from purchasing grains directly at the farm gate. Meanwhile, to ensure food affordability for urban consumers, the government used subsidies to keep retail grain prices consistently low, even below the procurement prices paid to farmers. These circulation and subsidy systems effectively eliminated the grey market for

[35] The majority of collectives were abolished towards the end of 1979.

[36] State Council of China. "*Document No. 137 of 1982. Circular on the Diligent Execution of All Operations Affecting Grain (Guowuyuan guanyu renzhen zuohao liangshi gongzuo de tongzhi).*" Beijing: State Council of China, November 28, 1982.

[37] From the beginning of reforms in 1980 to the agricultural reforms in 1993, the proportion of rice and wheat in China's total sown areas decreased from 42.8% to 39.9%. In contrast, the share of maize and soybean increased from 18.7% to 20.5%. By 2021, these figures had shifted to 31.7% for rice and wheat, and 30.7% for maize and soybeans, respectively. For detailed data, refer to the National Bureau of Statistics of China. National Data. Https://data.stats.gov.cn/english/easyquery.htm. Accessed January 15, 2024.

grain in China, positioning the government as the sole monopolist in the food sector.

This rural-urban dual-track food economy consequently created two isolated agricultural markets: one for rural producers and another for urban consumers. At the farm gate, rural households regained private use rights to farmland, granting them autonomy over production. In the cities, urban consumers benefited from subsidised food prices, which helped them accumulate purchasing power. However, a downside of this dual-track system was the disconnection of grain producers from the actual grain market, thereby stripping off the market's role in signalling production adjustments to rural grain producers. Moreover, as the Chinese government retained exclusive control over food pricing, it was able to procure grain at prices below market equilibrium and distribute the same grain at similarly reduced retail prices to urban consumers.[38] Therefore, this post-reform dual-track food system persisted in channelling large-scale rural surpluses to the industrial sector,[39] albeit at a reduced level of extraction before the reforms.

After the state grain monopoly was terminated in 2003, China's urban Engel's coefficient decreased from 57.5% in 1978 to 35.5% in 2003. Thus, the systemic grain crisis of 2003–2004[40] was primarily caused by the government's excessive extraction from the food sector. This crisis compelled the Chinese government to revise its agricultural and food security policies. Since 2005, the Hu-Wen administration abolished the food price scissors policy and began to subsidise grain producers.[41] Nevertheless, the rural-urban income gap remained a persistent issue due to the consistently low returns on agricultural production, which were a result of the low farm gate purchase prices for grain crops set by grain SOEs.

[38] Wang, Dewen, and Jikun, Huang. "An Analysis of China Farmers Grain Supply Impact under the Duel Price System (Shuangguizhi du xia zhongguo nonghu liangshi gongji fanying fenxi)." *Economic Research Journal (Jingji yanjiu)* 12 (2001): 55–65.

[39] Feng, Haifa, and Wei Li. "Quantitative Research on the Accumulative Funds Provided by Agriculture for China's Industrialisation (Woguo nongye wei gongyehua tigong zijin jilei de shuliang yanjiu)." *Economic Research Journal (Jingji yanjiu)* 9 (1993): 60–64.

[40] Du, Jane, and Cheng King. "Unravelling China's Food Security Puzzle, 1979–2008." *The China Quarterly* 235 (2018): 804–827.

[41] For further details, see the National Development and Reform Commission of China. ***Medium and Long-term Plan for National Food Security 2008–2020 (Guojia liangshi anquan zhongchangqi guihua gangyao 2008–2020 nian)***. Beijing: National Development and Reform Committee, November 13, 2008.

When food pricing was largely liberalised in the 2003 agricultural market reforms, grain SOEs were maintained as successors to the Grain Bureau. This change shaped a network with exclusive control over agricultural market, wherein each local grain SOE was granted unparalleled authority. Grain SOEs continued to dominate China's farm gate grain procurement, taking up the largest market share. As a result, the more peasants sold their grain to the SOEs, the less they benefited from the grain market sales. This dynamic highlighted a fundamental conflict between the interests of grain SOEs and the profitability of rural households' farming operations.

In the 2000s, as the government liberalised the rural-to-urban transfer of agricultural welfare, urban residential incomes began to rise sharply due to rapid industrial growth. This increase in urban purchasing power and the overall expansion of the economy enabled the Chinese government to resort its long-held food security responsibilities to the international commodity market. Consequently, the importance of rural welfare as a motive for ensuring food accessibility in China was substantially weakened and deprioritised.[42]

Food Security: Availability, Access and Affordability

Food security entails ensuring access to adequate supplies of nutritious and safe food to keep people healthy, active and productive. This, in turn, requires sufficient levels of both macronutrients and micronutrients to prevent malnutrition and undernourishment among the population. For a populous country, a fundamental challenge of food security is feeding its growing population.

From 1949 to 2022, the Chinese population nearly tripled, increasing from 0.5 billion to 1.4 billion. Therefore, in any case, food supply (or sufficiency) has consistently been the fundamental issue in China's food security challenges. In addition, with rising incomes, urban residents—especially in the eastern and coastal regions—have become increasingly affluent. While this has enhanced their purchasing power for food, it has also

[42] By 2023a, rural per person disposable income in China was 21,691 yuan, remained as low as 41.9% of that in the urban sector (51,821 yuan per person). These data were obtained from the National Bureau of Statistics of China. National Data. Https://data.stats.gov.cn/english/easyquery.htm. Accessed January 15, 2024.

exacerbated the disparity in food access between different demographic groups. In other words, China's pressing food security encompasses not only about food availability but also food access and affordability.

Compared to food availability, which primarily concerns food production, food access and affordability are more closely related to price and distribution. The distribution of income is a key factor shaping who can obtain the available food. More fundamentally, food access and affordability also involve the geographic and physical distribution of food (i.e. transportation and stockpiles).

However, fulfilling all aspects of food security is not easy. Despite the liberalisation of the food market, it is unlikely that China will deviate from its prioritisation on food issues. Although the state has reduced its food pricing rights and no longer monopolises food circulation, the Chinese government has maintained its strategic grain reserve system.[43] Decades of substantial economic growth have strengthened the financial position of the Chinese government, enabling it to re-establish an interventionist grain reserve system.

In principle, the grain reserve is designed to mitigate the unforeseen impacts of production shortfalls. Its primary goals are to address physical disruptions in food supplies,[44] stabilise grain market retail prices and protect the nation from food crises. The government has set a target for 2020

[43] In the mid-2010s, the Chinese government introduced three pivotal "red lines" designed to protect the agricultural sector: the "arable land red line," "water (environmental) resources red line" and the "grain reserve red line." Notably, the *Food Security Law of the PRC* (Draft) released in 2023 has re-emphasised two of these lines, namely the "arable land red line" and the "grain reserve red line." For more detailed information, please refer to Sinograin. *Sinograin: Constructing Three Security Lines of National Grain and Oil Reserves (Zhongchuliang: Gouzhu guojia liangyou chubei anquan santiao baozhang xian)*. Last modified 2014. Http://www.cngrain.com/Publish/news/201409/573580.shtml. Accessed August 15, 2019; and Xinhua News Agency. "China Mulls New Legislation to Safeguard Food Security." Published June 26, 2023b. Https://english.news.cn/20230626/4df7be3230204a449cd364c3e448ecff/c.html. Accessed January 15, 2024.

[44] China has officially announced that its grain reserves are sufficient to ensure a supply of essential food grains and oil products for up to 20 days in 36 major and medium-sized cities or regions, which are particularly vulnerable to frequent price fluctuations. For additional details, see the report by Xinhua News Agency. "China's Grain Stocks and Food Rations are Entirely Secure (Woguo liangshi kucun chongzu, kouliang juedui Anquan)." Published on June 26, 2023. Https://english.news.cn/20230626/4df7be3230204a449cd364c3e448ecff/c.html. Accessed January 15, 2024.

to increase China's grain reserve to an amount equal to 20% of annual domestic consumption. Wheat, rice and maize, the three major crops, are to constitute 85% of all strategic grain reserves.[45] Understandably, Beijing is focused on enhancing the efficiency and effectiveness of the grain reserve system.

The domestic output of these three major crops has grown steadily (Fig. 2.3). By 2021, the production of all three crops had either reached or approached their historical peaks.[46] Even when accounting for population growth, per capita grain output[47] has remained above China's food security threshold of 400 kilogrammes per person per year. This suggests that per capita food availability, based on domestic production, has been maintained at a stable and secure level.

It is evident that Beijing's persistent concern over food issues primarily stems from worries about inadequate food crop production.[48] However, if concerns about production shortfalls or the scarcity of grain availability are no longer significant reasons for anxiety about food security, the focus may shift to another crucial aspect: food accessibility. Specifically, this involves the price and affordability of grain for Chinese consumers.

[45] Sinograin. *Sinograin: Constructing Three Security Lines of National Grain and Oil Reserves (Zhongchuliang: Gouzhu guojia liangyou chubei anquan santiao baozhang xian).* Last modified 2014. Http://www.cngrain.com/Publish/news/201409/573580.shtml. Accessed August 15, 2019.

[46] In 2021, China achieved record-high production levels for its three major grain crops: wheat, producing 136.9 million tonnes; rice, with 212.8 million tonnes; and maize, reaching 272.6 million tonnes.

[47] In 2021, the per person grain output in China was 483.4 kilogrammes per year, exceeding the country's food security threshold of 400 kilogrammes per person per year.

[48] Since mid-2012, agricultural production has regained its position as the foremost priority in annual national economic plans. The central government has demonstrated a steadfast commitment to food self-sufficiency. In late December 2013, members of the CCP standing committee emphasised at an agricultural work meeting that "grain self-sufficiency must be ensured, food rations must be kept absolutely safe, and farmland must strictly adhere to the arable land red line." This commitment was further highlighted when, on January 20th, 2014, Central Document No. 1 was issued, reiterating food security as a principal policy objective of Beijing. For additional information, refer to the Central Committee of the CCP and the State Council of China. "*Document No. 1 of 2014. Circular of the Central Committee of CCP and State Council on Issuing the 'Opinions on Comprehensively Deepening Rural Reform and Accelerating Agricultural Modernization' (Zhonggong zhongyang, guowuyuan yinfa guanyu quanmian shenhua nongcun gaige jiakuai tuijin nongye xiandaihua de ruogan yijian).*" Beijing: Central Committee of the CCP and the State Council of China Document, January 20, 2014.

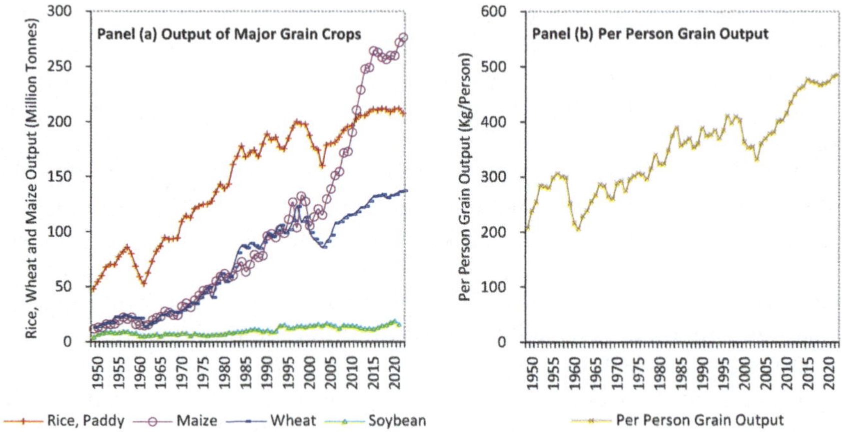

Fig. 2.3 Output of major grain crops and per person grain output since 1949

Since 1949, a low selling price for grain was associated with strengthened food accessibility, provided the state maintained a monopoly over the grain circulation system and could ensure a sufficient surplus from agricultural production. However, after 2003, the situation changed. With the market determining grain procurement pricing,[49] the state retained the authority to regulate prices to ensure that urban consumers could still afford food.[50] Instead, the Chinese government turned to the grain reserve system as an alternative means to intervene in the market and stabilise food prices.[51] This shift highlights the significance of grain reserves in

[49] Refer to the State Council of China. "*Document No. 17 of 2004. Opinions of the State Council on Further Deepening the Reform to the Grain Distribution System (Guowuyuan guanyu jinyibu shenhua liangshi liutong tizhi gaige de yijian).*" Beijing: State Council of China, May 23, 2004.

[50] Following the grain supply crisis in 2003, the Chinese government transferred the authority to determine food prices to the market, retaining only the right to set protective pricing for major grain crops.

[51] Concerns about China's food security were renewed in 2008, highlighted by a document from the National Development and Reform Commission. More information can be found in the National Development and Reform Commission of China. ***Medium and Long-term Plan for National Food Security 2008–2020 (Guojia liangshi anquan zhongchangqi guihua gangyao 2008–2020 nian)***. Beijing: National Development and Reform Committee, November 13, 2008.

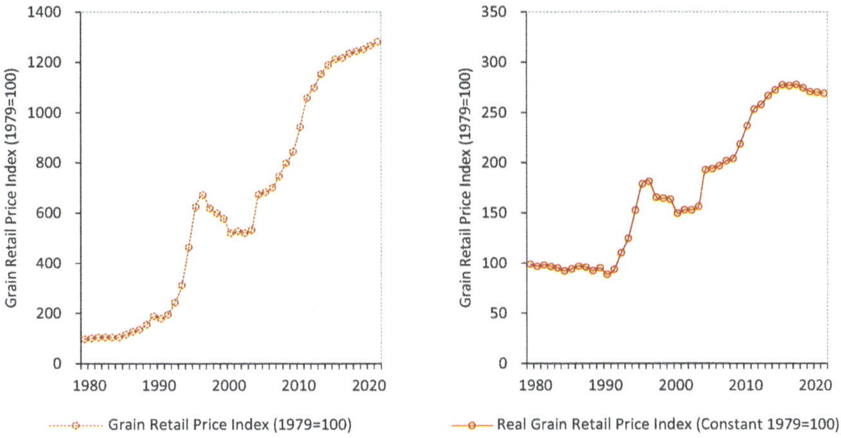

Fig. 2.4 Grain retail price indices

understanding the gradual but consistent rise in food prices since 2008 (as shown in Fig. 2.4).[52]

Beyond market intervention through grain reserve management, safeguarding food accessibility can also be achieved by increasing disposable income. As a household income grows, the proportion of spending on grains and other essential food items decreases. As indicated in Table 2.2, Engel's coefficients[53] in both urban and rural China were halved between 1979 and 2021.[54] Consequently, even significant increases in grain prices have a limited influence on individual food demand, provided that

[52] From the beginning of reforms until the liberalisation of the food sector in 2004, the retail price of grain experienced a spike during 1994–1996, as shown in Fig. 2.4. This surge was primarily attributed to the government's increased control over the farming and circulation of grain crops. On the one hand, the grain procurement price was raised to encourage production. On the other hand, in 1993, the state terminated the urban food coupon system and significantly reduced state subsidies for urban food consumption. As a result, food grain retail prices peaked in the mid-1990s due to the 1993 and 1994 grain reforms.

[53] The Engel's coefficient describes a consistent phenomenon observed across households: as income increases, the proportion of income spent on food decreases. This occurs even though the total amount spent on food may increase.

[54] From 1978 to 2021, urban Engel's coefficients decreased from 57.5% to 28.6%, while rural Engel's coefficients fell from 67.7% to 32.7% during the same period.

Table 2.2 Per capita disposal income and Engel's coefficients

Year	*National-level Engle's coefficients (%)*	*Urban*		*Rural*	
		Urban per capita disposable income (Yuan)	*Urban Engle's coefficients (%)*	*Rural per capita disposable income (Yuan)*	*Rural Engle's coefficients (%)*
	(1)	(2)	(3)	(4)	(5)
1978	63.9	343.4	57.5	134.0	67.7
1983	59.4	564.6	59.2	310.0	59.4
1988	52.8	1180.2	51.4	545.0	54.0
1993	54.0	2577.4	50.1	922.0	58.1
1994	54.1	3496.2	49.9	1221.0	58.9
1998	48.0	5425.1	44.2	2171.0	53.2
2003	38.1	8472.2	35.5	2690.0	43.9
2004	38.8	9421.6	35.8	3027.0	45.3
2008	36.3	15,780.8	34.5	4999.0	40.9
2013	31.2	26,467.0	30.1	9430.0	34.1
2019	28.2	42,359.0	27.6	16,021.0	30.0
2021	29.8	47,412.0	28.6	18,931.0	32.7

Source: Department of Comprehensive Statistics of National Bureau of Statistics of China. *China Compendium of Statistics 1949–2008 (Xin Zhongguo 60 nian tongji ziliao huibian)*. Beijing: China Statistics Press (Zhongguo tongji chuban she), 2010; National Bureau of Statistics of China. *China Statistical Yearbook (Zhongguo tongji nianjian)*. Beijing: China Statistics Press (Zhongguo tongji chuban she), 1981–2023 editions; National Bureau of Statistics of China. National Data. Https://data.stats.gov.cn/english/easyquery.htm. Accessed January 15, 2024

household income growth outpaces price increases. From 1979 to 2021, the per capita disposable income of urban Chinese residents surged 137-fold in nominal terms (Table 2.2, Column 2), while the urban Engel's coefficient dropped from 57.5% to 28.6% (Table 2.2, Column 3). Thus, expenditure on food consumption has become less of a financial burden for Chinese households.

Nevertheless, the declining Engel's coefficients primarily reflect the improved purchasing power of the Chinese Yuan. While a higher income level enhances the average financial capability of individual Chinese citizens to afford food, the fast-growing demand for animal protein-rich products has also lowered the importance of plant-based foods (i.e. food grain in Fig. 2.5, Panels a) in the Chinese diet. Among all sources of animal protein, meat, including poultry, remains China's preferred main source (Fig. 2.5, Panels b). Over the past decade, the country has

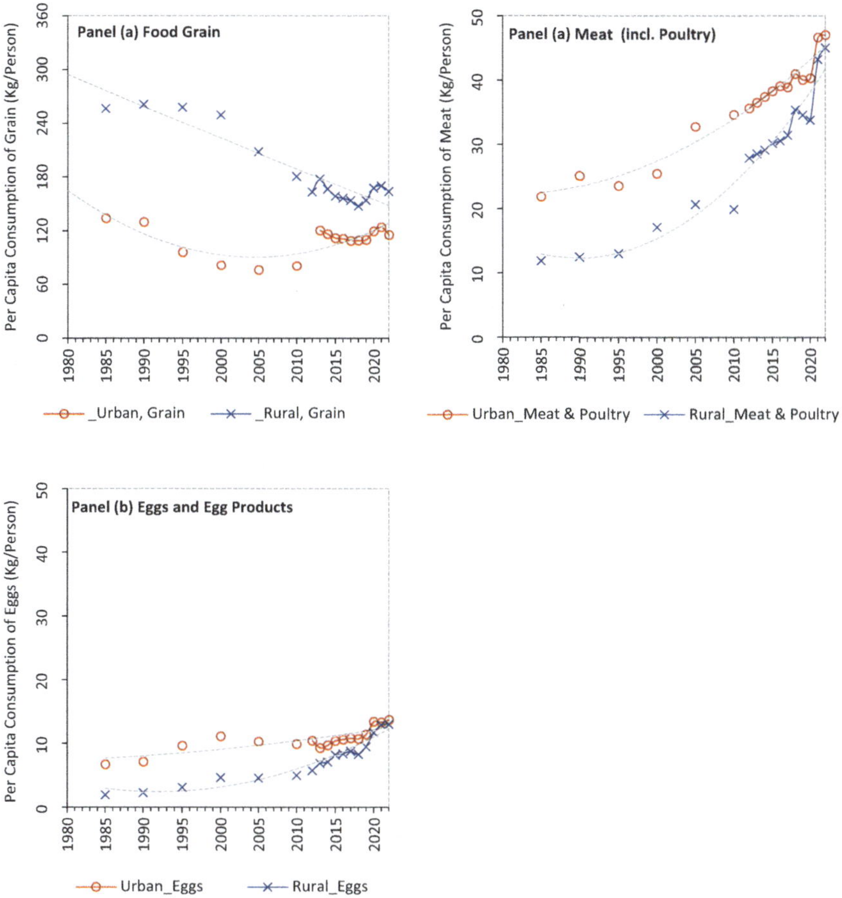

Fig. 2.5 Per capita consumption of grain and major animal protein sources

experienced a significant structural change in food consumption, with per person meat intake increasing by 44.6%,[55] according to the *China Statistical Yearbooks.*

[55] From 2013 to 2022, per capita consumption of pork, beef, lamb and poultry combined increased from 29.4 kilogrammes to 42.5 kilogrammes, representing a 44.6% rise over the decade. For detailed data, see the National Bureau of Statistics of China. *China Statistical Yearbook (Zhongguo tongji nianjian)*. Beijing: China Statistics Press (Zhongguo tongji chuban she), 1981–2023 editions.

Such a structural change implies that the price elasticities of demand for different food varieties have changed alongside China's income transition. Food varieties with stable elasticities are expected to pose new challenges for future food issues in China. Following Xiao and Hu,[56] Table 2.3 illustrates the evolution of price elasticities of demand for grain and major animal protein sources in China from 1995 to 2019. While grain and egg consumption remain inelastic (Table 2.3, Columns 1–2 and 5–6), the price elasticity of demand for meet has declined, approaching a unitary level of "one" (Table 2.3, Columns 3–4). Given the recent significant slowdown in the Chinese economy, the unit price elasticity of meat suggests that China's annual per person meat consumption may have reached a plateau.

Furthermore, when examining the structure of meat consumption using 2021 levels as an example, China's per capita meat intake was 41.4 kilogrammes, consisting 25.2 kilogrammes of pork, 12.3 kilogrammes of poultry, and 3.9 kilogrammes of beef and lamb combined.[57] According to

Table 2.3 Price elasticity of demand for grain, meat and egg products in China

Year	*Price elasticity of demand (%)*					
	Grain		*Meat (incl. poultry)*		*Eggs and egg products*	
	Urban	*Rural*	*Urban*	*Rural*	*Urban*	*Rural*
	(1)	(2)	(3)	(4)	(5)	(6)
1995–2000	0.04	0.44	1.27	2.61	0.52	−0.26
2001–2006	−0.05	0.29	1.27	2.29	0.18	−0.19
2007–2012	−0.08	0.06	1.27	2.14	−0.08	0.06
2015–2019	−0.11	−0.06	1.25	1.61	−0.05	0.28

Source: Xiao Xue, and Bingchuan Hu. "Analysis on Food Consumption of Urban and Rural Residents—Based on QUAIDS and EASI Model (Zhong chengxiang jumin shipin xiaofei fenxi—jiyu QUAIDS moxing he EASI moxing)." *World Agriculture (Shijie nongye)* 7 (2002): 67–81

[56] See Tables 6 and 7 in the article by Xiao Xue, and Bingchuan Hu. "Analysis on Food Consumption of Urban and Rural Residents—Based on QUAIDS and EASI Model (Zhong chengxiang jumin shipin xiaofei fenxi—jiyu QUAIDS moxing he EASI moxing)." *World Agriculture (Shijie nongye)* 7 (2002): 67–81.

[57] The structure of China's meat consumption has remained stable over the past decade. Pork consumption accounted for an average of about 62.2% of total meat consumption, poultry for 28.5%, and beef and lamb for about 9.3%.

the conversion rates released by the United States Grain Council,[58] the 2021 level of meat consumption necessitates China to produce an additional 169.1 kilogrammes of grain per person for fodder use, which is 42.3% higher than the current self-sufficiency threshold of 400 kilogrammes per person per year.

Hence, the government's heightened concern over food security after 2008 cannot be fully explained by either apprehension about staple food output shortages or fears about decline in food affordability.[59] In fact, the increasing demand of fodder grain has already posed a great challenge to China's grain production.

In addition, the grain reserves have also seen expansion. Over the past decade, efforts to reinforce the reserve system have encountered difficulties. The government established procurement systems to maintain these reserves, which inflated domestic prices and encouraged imports (e.g. maize temporary storage policy[60]). These actions necessitated substantial government spending to manage the burgeoning grain reserve system, particularly as grain output reached historical highs. Importantly, the grain reserve system alone has not addressed issues of food access and affordability. This is because disposable household income has increased more rapidly than food prices, ensuring continued food accessibility and affordability for the Chinese population. A lingering question is how Beijing will address the rising demand for fodder grain, which is becoming increasingly crucial for China's food security.

[58] According to the United States Grains Council, every kilogramme of pork requires 5.8 kilogrammes of fodder grains, beef requires 11.9 kilogrammes and poultry requires 3.0 kilogrammes. Since the conversion rate for lamb is unavailable and its consumption is relatively small in China, the conversion rate used for lamb is based on that for beef. For detailed conversion methods, refer to the United States Grains Council. "Conversion of Meat Exports to Corn Equivalents." Https://grains.org/wp-content/uploads/2018/02/Conversion-of-meat-exports-to-corn-equivalents.pdf. Accessed July 15, 2024.

[59] Xi Jinping emphasised, "In any situation, the bowls of the Chinese must rest in our own hands. Our bowls should be filled mainly with Chinese grain." This declaration underscores the importance he places on China maintaining control over its food security. For insights into Xi Jinping's perspectives on China's food security issues, refer to the Party Literature Research Centre of the Communist Party of China. *Excerpts from Xi Jinping's Exposition on National Food Security*. Beijing: Central Party Literature Press, 2023.

[60] Chapter 4 will detail the specifics of the maize temporary storage policy.

References

Central Committee of the CCP and the State Council of China. "*Document No. 1 of 2014. Circular of the Central Committee of CCP and State Council on Issuing the 'Opinions on Comprehensively Deepening Rural Reform and Accelerating Agricultural Modernisation' (Zhonggong zhongyang, guowuyuan yinfa guanyu quanmian shenhua nongcun gaige jiakuai tuijin nongye xiandaihua de ruogan yijian).*" Beijing: Central Committee of the CCP and the State Council of China, January 20, 2014.

Central Committee of the CCP. "*Document No. 1 of 2004. Opinions of the Central Committee and the State Council Concerning Several Policies on Promoting the Increase of Farmers' (Income Zhonggong zhongyang, guowuyuan guanyu cujin nongmin zengjia shouru ruogan zhengce de yijian).*" Beijing: Central Committee of the CCP and the State Council of China, December 31, 2003.

Central Committee of the CCP. "*Document No. 1 of 2005. Opinions of the Central Committee and the State Council Concerning Several Policies on Further Strengthening Rural Works and Promoting the Comprehensive Agricultural Productivities (Zhonggong zhongyang, guowuyuan guanyu jin yibu jiaqiang nongcun gongzuo tigao nongye zonghe shengchan nengli ruogan zhengce de yijian).*" Beijing: Central Committee of the CCP and the State Council of China, December 31, 2004.

Central Committee of the CCP. "*Document No. 1 of 2006. Opinions of the Central Committee and the State Council on Promoting the Construction of the New Socialist Country (Zhonggong zhongyang, guowuyuan guanyu tuijin shehui zhuyi xin nongcun jianshe de ruogan yijian).*" Beijing: Central Committee of the CCP and the State Council of China, December 31, 2005.

Central Committee of the CCP. "*Document No. 1 of 2007. Opinions of the Central Committee and the State Council on Actively Developing Modern Agriculture and Steady Promoting the Construction of the New Socialist Country (Zhonggong zhongyang, guowuyuan guanyu jiji fazhan xiandai nongye zhashi tuijin shehui zuyi xin nongce jianshe de ruogan yijian).*" Beijing: Central Committee of the CCP and the State Council of China, December 31, 2006.

Central Committee of the CCP. "*Document No.1. 1985. Ten Policies of the Central Committee and the State Council for Further Enlivening the Rural Economy (Zhonggong zhongyang guowuyuan guanyu jinyibu huoyue nongcun jingji de shixiang zhengce).*" Beijing: CCP Central Committee, January 1, 1985.

Department of Comprehensive Statistics of National Bureau of Statistics of China. *China Compendium of Statistics 1949–2008 (Xin Zhongguo 60 nian tongji ziliao huibian)*. Beijing: China Statistics Press (Zhongguo tongji chuban she), 2010.

Du, Jane and Kent Deng. "Getting Food Prices Right: The State versus the Market in Reforming China, 1979–2006." *European Review of Economic History* 21 (2017): 302–325.

Du, Jane, and Cheng King. "Unravelling China's Food Security Puzzle, 1979–2008." *The China Quarterly* 235 (2018): 804–827.

Fan, Qimiao, and Peter Nolan (eds.). *China's Economic Reforms: The Costs and Benefits of Incrementalism*. Basingstoke: Palgrave Macmillan, 1994.

Feng, Haifa, and Wei Li. "Quantitative Research on the Accumulative Funds Provided by Agriculture for China's Industrialisation (Woguo nongye wei gongyehua tigong zijin jilei de shuliang yanjiu)." *Economic Research Journal (Jingji yanjiu)* 9 (1993): 60–64.

Lardy, Nicholas R. *Agriculture in China's Modern Economic Development*. Cambridge: Cambridge University Press, 1983.

Lin, Justin Y. "An Economic Theory of Institutional Change: Induced and Imposed Change." *Cato Journal* 9 (1989): 1–33.

Lin, Justin Y. "The Household Responsibility System Reform and the Adoption of Hybrid Rice in China." *Journal of Development Economics* 36 (1991): 353–372.

McMillan, John, John Whalley, and Lijing Zhu. "The Impact of China's Economic Reforms on Agricultural Productivity Growth." *Journal of Political Economy* 97 (1989): 781–807.

National Bureau of Statistics of China. *China Statistical Yearbook (Zhongguo tongji nianjian)*. Beijing: China Statistics Press (Zhongguo tongji chuban she), 1981–2023 editions.

National Bureau of Statistics of China. National Data. Https://data.stats.gov.cn/english/easyquery.htm. Accessed January 15, 2024.

National Development and Reform Commission of China. *Medium and Long-term Plan for National Food Security 2008–2020 (Guojia liangshi anquan zhongchangqi guihua gangyao 2008–2020 nian)*. Beijing: National Development and Reform Committee, 13 November 2008.

Party Literature Research Centre of the Communist Party of China. *Excerpts from Xi Jinping's Exposition on National Food Security*. Beijing: Central Party Literature Press, 2023.

Second Session of the Ninth Standing Committee of the National People's Congress of China. *Agriculture Law of the People's Republic of China (Zhonghua renmin gongheguo nongye fa)*. Beijing: National People's Congress, July 2, 1993.

Sinograin. *Sinograin: Constructing Three Security Lines of National Grain and Oil Reserves (Zhongchuliang: Gouzhu guojia liangyou chubei anquan santiao baozhang xian)*. Last modified 2014. Http://www.cngrain.com/Publish/news/201409/573580.shtml. Accessed August 15, 2019.

State Council of China. "*Decree No. 407 of 2004a. Regulations on Administration of Grain Distribution (Liangshi liutong guanli tiaoli).*" Beijing: State Council of China, May 26, 2004a.

State Council of China. "*Document No. 137 of 1982. Circular on the Diligent Execution of All Operations Affecting Grain (Guowuyuan guanyu renzhen zuohao liangshi gongzuo de tongzhi).*" Beijing: State Council of China, November 28, 1982.

State Council of China. "*Document No. 17 of 2004. Opinions of the State Council on Further Deepening the Reform to the Grain Distribution System (Guowuyuan guanyu jinyibu shenhua liangshi liutong tizhi gaige de yijian).*" Beijing: State Council of China, May 23, 2004b.

State Council of China. "*Document No. 32 of 1994. Circular of the State Council on the Further Reform of Grain Purchase and Selling System (Guowuyuan guanyu shenhua liangshi gouxiao tizhi gaige de tongzhi).*" Beijing: State Council of China, May 9, 1994.

State Council of China. "*Document No. 9 of 1993. Circular of the State Council on Speeding up Reform of the Grain Circulation System (Guowuyuan guanyu jiakuai liangshi liutong tizhi gaige de tongzhi).*" Beijing: State Council of China, February 15, 1993.

State Council of China. "*Document No.15 of 1992. Decisions of the State Council on Increasing the State Monopoly Selling Price of Grain (Guowuyuan guanyu tigao liangshi tongxiao jiage de jueding).*" Beijing: State Council of China, March 6, 1992.

State Council of the China. "*Decree No. 244 of 1998. Regulations on Grain Purchase (Liangshi shougou tiaoli).*" Beijing: State Council of China, June 6, 1998a.

State Council of the China. "*Document No. 15 of 1998. Decision of the State Council on Further Reform over the Grain Circulation System (Guowuyuan guanyu jinyibu shenhua liangshi liutong tizhi gaige de jueding).*" Beijing: State Council of the China, May 10, 1998b.

United States Department of Agriculture. *International Agricultural Total Factor Productivity Indices, 1961–2021.* Https://www.ers.usda.gov/data-products/international-agricultural-productivity. Accessed January 15, 2024.

United States Grains Council. "Conversion of Meat Exports to Corn Equivalents." Https://grains.org/wp-content/uploads/2018/02/Conversion-of-meat-exports-to-corn-equivalents.pdf. Accessed July 15, 2024.

Wang, Dewen, and Jikun, Huang. "An Analysis of China Farmers Grain Supply Impact under the Duel Price System (Shuangguizhi du xia zhongguo nonghu liangshi gongji fanying fenxi)." *Economic Research Journal (Jingji yanjiu)* 12 (2001): 55–65.

Xiao Xue, and Bingchuan Hu. "Analysis on Food Consumption of Urban and Rural Residents—Based on QUAIDS and EASI Model (Zhong chengxiang jumin shipin xiaofei fenxi—jiyu QUAIDS moxing he EASI moxing)." *World Agriculture (Shijie nongye)* 7 (2002): 67–81.

Xinhua News Agency. "China Mulls New Legislation to Safeguard Food Security." Published June 26, 2023a. Https://english.news.cn/20230626/4df7be3230204a449cd364c3e448ecff/c.html. Accessed January 15, 2024.

Xinhua News Agency. "China's Grain Stocks and Food Rations are Entirely Secure (Woguo liangshi kucun chongzu, kouliang juedui Anquan)." Published on 26 June 2023b. Https://english.news.cn/20230626/4df7be3230204a449cd364c3e448ecff/c.html. Accessed January 15, 2024.

CHAPTER 3

Grain Ration Needs, Fodder Grain and Import Dependence

Abstract This chapter explores China's dependence on food imports, focussing on fodder grain imports before and after the onset of the Sino-US economic conflict. Following the announcement by the United States of tariffs on Chinese imports, China retaliated by imposing a significant 179% tariff on the American sorghum. Additional levies were also applied to dried distillers' grains with solubles, fish-bone power and fish meals. While considerable attention was given to the impact on American farmers, China's livestock industry faced serious repercussions due to its substantial reliance on fodder-based agricultural imports from the United States. To this day, the United States remains the most crucial fodder exporter to China. In an effort to lessen China's reliance on the United States, China is expected to adjust its fodder commodity imports, balancing between protein varieties and energy forage crops.

Keywords Food grain • Fodder grain • Maize • Soybeans • The United States • Brazil • Import dependence • Terms of trade • Labour-intensive industries • Land-intensive agricultural products • Harmonised system code • Energy forage crops • Protein forage crops • Prepared fodder • The Sino-US trade war

J. Du, *Farmland, Farming and Food in the National Economy of China, 1947–2020*, Palgrave Studies in Economic History,
https://doi.org/10.1007/978-3-031-70027-9_3

Production-Consumption Gap of Grain Crops

A closer examination of China's domestic grain output and consumption patterns reveals that the production of the country's staple food grains—namely rice and wheat—closely matched the total consumption demand. In 2021, rice consumption was recorded at 156.3 million tonnes, compared to a domestic output of 212.8 million tonnes. Similarly, wheat consumption reached 148.8 million tonnes, which exceeded the domestic production of 136.9 million tonnes. More broadly, the latest report of the Food and Agriculture Organisation indicates that in 2021, China's per capita cereal output surpassed the global average by 59.9 kilogrammes (see Fig. 3.1).[1]

As of 2021, China's consumption of food grain reached approximately 250 million tonnes, with fodder grain allocation at 270 million tonnes and industrial use at 160 million tonnes.[2] Consequently, the demand for fodder grain has had a more significant impact on China's food security than the need for rationed food. Among all major grain crops, maize and soybeans have served as the primary sources of fodder grain. Since 1979, domestic maize production has experienced the fastest growth, averaging about 8.4% annually.[3] This growth is notable, considering that maize constitutes the basis of China's fodder crops, accounting for approximately 70% of its consumption for fodder grain use in recent years.[4] However,

[1] In 2021, the per capita maize output in China was approximately 193.4 kilogrammes. While this figure is comparable to the global average of 153.4 kilogrammes, it falls short compared to the per capita output in the United States (1,156.5 kilogrammes), Argentina (1,321.3 kilogrammes) and Brazil (413.4 kilogrammes). This data was sourced from the Food and Agriculture Organisation of the United Nations. *FAOSTAT, Crops and Livestock Products*. Https://www.fao.org/faostat/en/#data/QCL. Accessed January 15, 2024; and World Bank. World Development Indicators. Washington: World Bank. Https://datacatalog.worldbank.org/dataset/world-development-indicators. Accessed January 15, 2024.

[2] *Guangming Daily*. "Promoting the 'Three Transformations' to Build a New Development Structure of National Food Security (Tuidong 'san ge zhuanbian' goujian guojia liangshi anquan fazhan xin de geju)." Published on 11 May 2022. Https://epaper.gmw.cn/gmrb/html/2022-05/11/nw.D110000gmrb_20220511_1-06.htm. Accessed January 15, 2024.

[3] The growth rates of maize are calculated based on the average annual increase from 1979 to 2021.

[4] *Economic Daily*. 2022. "Fodder Grain Supply Affects National Food Security (Siliao liang gongji guanhu guojia liangshi anquan)." Published on 7 July 2023. Http://paper.ce.cn/pad/content/202307/07/content_277029.html. Accessed January 15, 2024.

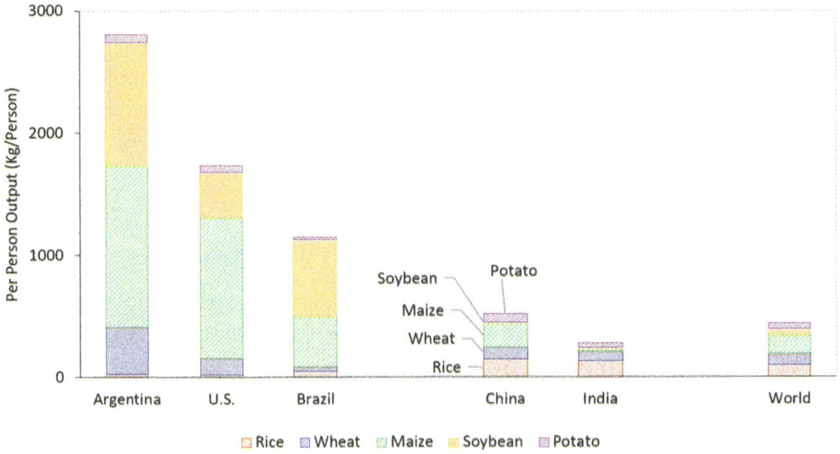

Fig. 3.1 Per capita output of grain crops in selected countries, 2021 level

China has faced challenges with soybeans, its major oil crop. In 2021, domestic production stood at 19.6 million tonnes, which was significantly lower than the domestic consumption of 108.7 million tonnes.[5] Furthermore, per person soybean output in China was only 116.4 kilogrammes, much lower than the global average of 47.1 kilogrammes (Fig. 3.1).[6]

Although China's agriculture has demonstrated strong productivity growth, as evidenced by a total grain output of 682.9 million tonnes in 2021—which suggests the country's capability to meet its population's grain needs—concerns remain due to the uneven distribution of output and consumption across major crops. The recent strong performance of maize, for example, can largely be attributed to its expanding sown area, a

[5] Data was collected from an article in the *Economic Daily*. 2022. "Fodder Grain Supply Affects National Food Security (Siliao liang gongji guanhu guojia liangshi anquan)." Published on 7 July 2023. Http://paper.ce.cn/pad/content/202307/07/content_277029.html. Accessed January 15, 2024.

[6] According to the Food and Agriculture Organisation, in 2021, per person soybean output was reported to be 363.8 kilogrammes in the United States, 1,008.9 kilogrammes in Argentina and 630.5 kilogrammes in Brazil.

consequence of reallocating farmland from wheat and rice, rather than increases in yield. From 1979 to 2021, the sown area for maize increased at a yearly rate of 2.7%, in contrast to the shrinking acreage allocated to wheat (−0.5%) and rice (−0.3%).[7] Addressing the challenge of supporting the dietary transition of an increasingly urbanised population, without compromising the cultivation of staple food crops, is imperative for China.

Food Imports by Product Categories

The escalating demand for fodder grains in the animal industry has exceeded domestic production levels in China, prompting the government to seek solutions to bridge the demand-supply gap. Four potential strategies have been identified to alleviate the pressure on fodder grain resources: (1) increasing direct imports of animal products, (2) expanding overseas farmland leasing to boost fodder grain production for export to China, (3) transitioning to maize cultivation on lands currently allocated for staple food grains and cash crops, and (4) increasing the importation of fodder grains.

- *The first option* involves increasing the direct importation of animal products, necessitating China's transition from a net grain exporter to a significant importer of meat products. While this approach could quickly reduce the pressure on fodder grain production, it has the drawback of exposing the domestic consumption market to international price shocks in the animal protein food products.
- *The second option* entails leasing additional overseas farmland to increase fodder grain production for export to China. This would require domestic agricultural enterprises to expand their operations internationally. The feasibility of this option depends greatly on the socio-political conditions in the host countries. Additionally, the inherent challenges of agriculture, such as weather variability and extended payback periods, typically render this option less favourable due to the increased investment risks associated with overseas agricultural ventures.

[7] Sown area data for rice, wheat and maize was collected from the National Bureau of Statistics of China. National Data. Https://data.stats.gov.cn/english/easyquery.htm. Accessed January 15, 2024.

- *The third option* involves expanding the domestic sown area of fodder grain at the potential expense of reducing the cultivation of staple food grains and cash crops. However, this strategy hinges on a substantial policy shift. Unless the government revises its goal of 95% self-sufficiency in staple foods through domestic production and resorts to the global commodity market to bridge the shortfall, the limited availability of farmland makes it increasingly difficult to switch from food grain to fodder grain cultivation.[8]
- *The fourth option* involves augmenting the domestic supply by boosting the quantity of directly imported fodder crops, which appears straightforward and feasible. Although there is some flexibility in adjusting fodder grain imports based to demand conditions, the primary ingredients in China's animal fodder industry are maize and soybean meals, catering to the poultry and pork industries, respectively. However, China's growing demand in international commodity markets has raised global concerns due to its broad implications for the food security of many countries beyond China itself.

Starting in the early 1990s, China has emerged as a major importer of grain products, with maize imports being particularly notable. The magnitude of China's importation has seen a substantial surge in recent years. Figure 3.2 illustrates China's involvement in the commodity maize market, highlighting the associated price volatility over the past 60 years. China's growing demand has raised international concerns, as evidenced

[8] To safeguard the designated 1.8 billion mu of arable land for major staple food crops and prevent its diversion for industrial purposes, the government contemplated measures to restrict the industrial use of maize. This commitment to safeguarding farmland was highlighted by the Ministry of Agriculture's emphasis on using a special fund for farmland protection, as outlined on January 15, 2018. Further details can be found in the documents issued by the Ministry of Agriculture and Rural Affairs of China. *Circular of the Ministry of Agriculture and Rural Affairs on Issuing the "Measures of Managing Special Fund for Protecting Arable Land Quality" (Nongyebu guanyu yinfa "gengdi zhiliang baohu zhuanxiang zijin guanli banfa" de tongzhi)*. Beijing: Ministry of Agriculture and Rural Affairs of China, January 15, 2018; National Development and Reform Commission of China. *Urgent Notice on Strengthening the Management of the Construction of Maize Processing Projects (Guanyu jiaqiang yumi jiagong xiangmu jianshe guanli de jinji tongzhi)*. Beijing: National Development and Reform Commission, 2006.

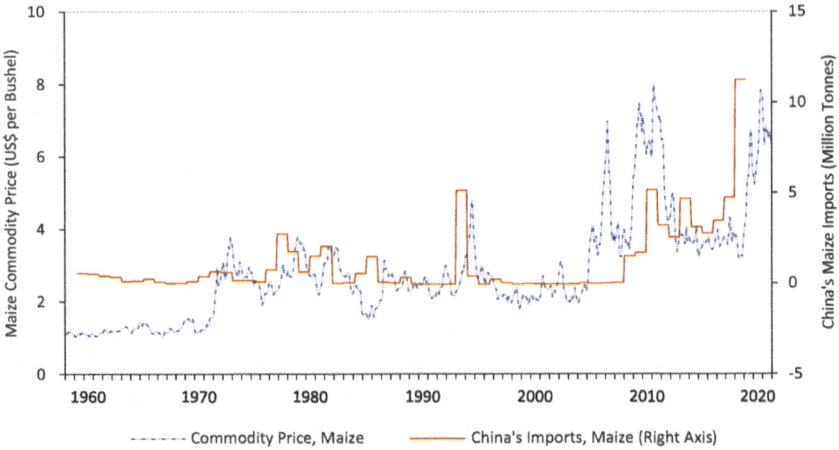

Fig. 3.2 Price of commodity maize and China's imports

by a 197.0% increase in commodity maize prices from 2003 to 2022.[9] This surge in demand, driven by the needs of both the animal fodder sector and biofuel production, has outpaced the growth in domestic output. In an effort to prevent the diversion of farmland from cereal crops, the government has contemplated measures to limit the industrial use of maize.[10]

In fact, China's growing demand for most crops is expected to outpace domestic production growth in the coming years. In 2021, the total trade value of agricultural products in China reached US$304.2 billion, marking a 23.2% increase from 2020, with net imports amounting to US$135.5 billion.[11] During the period of 2021–2022, China remained the world's

[9] From 2003 to 2022, the annual commodity price of maize increased from US$2.3 per bushel to US$6.9, marking a total increase of 197.0%. For more detailed data on maize commodity prices, please refer to Macrotrends. *Corn Prices—59 Year Historical Chart*. Https://www.macrotrends.net/2532/corn-prices-historical-chart-data. Accessed January 15, 2024.

[10] National Development and Reform Commission of China. *Urgent Notice on Strengthening the Management of the Construction of Maize Processing Projects (Guanyu jiaqiang yumi jiagong xiangmu jianshe guanli de jinji tongzhi)*. Beijing: National Development and Reform Commission, 2006.

[11] Ministry of Agriculture of China. "*China's Import and Export of Agricultural Products in 2021 (2021 Nian woguo nongchanpin jin chukou qingkuang)*." Published January 27, 2022. Http://www.moa.gov.cn/ztzl/nybrl/rlxx/202201/t20220127_6387781.htm. Accessed January 15, 2024.

leading importer of soybeans, maize, wheat, sorghum and DDGS,[12] which are primarily used as fodder. Table 3.1 presents the structure of China's imports of agricultural products for the year 2021.

China's dependence on trade for specific agricultural products, including grain crops and oilseeds, becomes evident when examining the trade volume and the share of trade in domestic supply for each product. Following the data published by China's National Bureau of Statistics and the Ministry of Agriculture, the net imports of major agricultural products for 2021 can be categorised as follows:

- **Cereals:** China was a net exporter of cereal crops until 2009. However, there has been a rapid increase in cereal imports since 2010, reaching a peak of 65.4 million tonnes in 2021. The net import of cereals in 2021 was 62.1 million tonnes, with major suppliers including the United States, Ukraine, Argentina, Canada, France and Australia. The decrease in cereal imports from 2016 to 2019 was due to the termination of China's temporary storage policy for maize, which led to increased use of local maize as fodder grain.

Table 3.1 Imports of selected agricultural products in 2021

	Import (Million tonnes)		*Import (Million tonnes)*
	(1)		(2)
Cereals	65.4	*Edible oilseeds*	102.1
Sorghum	11.0	Soybean	96.5
Barley	12.5	Rapeseed	2.6
Wheat	9.8		
Maize	28.4	*Edible vegetable oils*	10.4
Rice, paddy	5.0	Palm oil	4.7
Cassava (dried)	3.5	*Fodder meals*	3.1
Sugar	5.7	DDGS	0.3

Source: Ministry of Agriculture and Rural Affairs of China. "***China's Import and Export of Agricultural Products in 2021 (2021 Nian woguo nongchanpin jinchukou)***." Published January 18, 2023. Http://www.moa.gov.cn/ztzl/nybrl/rlxx/202201/t20220127_6387781.htm. Accessed January 15, 2024; National Bureau of Statistics of China. National Data. Https://data.stats.gov.cn/english/easyquery.htm. Accessed January 15, 2024

[12] Distillers grains (and solubles) are available in two main forms: wet and dried (WDG[S] and DDG[S]). The dried form offers several advantages, including easier handling, reduced transportation costs and an extended shelf life, which allows for longer storage periods.

- **Edible vegetable oils:** China has long faced a shortage of edible vegetable oils, with net imports exceeding five million tonnes annually since the mid-2000s, peaking at 8.4 million tonnes in 2012. In 2021, China's total imports of edible vegetable oils reached 11.3 million tonnes, with palm oil accounting for the largest share at 56.4%, followed by rapeseed oil at 19.0%, soybean oil at 9.9% and peanut oil at 2.5%.[13] China's primary trading partners for vegetable oils include Indonesia, Malaysia, Russia, Ukraine and Brazil.
- **Oilseeds:** The main oil crops imported by China include soybeans, rapeseeds, peanuts and sunflower seeds. The surge in the import volume of oilseeds is attributed to both the domestic shortage of vegetable oil and the demand for protein sources in animal fodder, driven by the improving living standard of the Chinese people. In 2021, China imported 102.1 million tonnes of oilseeds, with soybeans constituting the majority at 96.5 million tonnes. The second largest imported variety was rapeseed, at approximately 2.6 million tonnes. Brazil, the United States and Argentina are the primary sources of China's oilseed imports.
- **Fodder meals (DDGS):** In addition to domestic production, China has engaged in substantial trade of fodder meals, which are crucial protein sources for animal fodder, such as soybean meals, rapeseed meals and DDGS. Before the late 2000s, the country was a net exporter of fodder meals. However, the rapid increase in DDGS imports since 2010 transformed the country into a major net importer of fodder meals. China's net import of DDGS peaked at 6.8 million tonnes in 2015, then dropped to 3.1 million tonnes in 2016 and further declined to 0.2 million tonnes in 2021. This reduction was a consequence of the cancellation of the domestic temporary storage policy for maize in April 2016. China's largest trade partner for DDGS was the United States. Unlike DDGS, soybean meals were mostly produced domestically using imported soybeans.
- **Sugar and cassava:** China's net sugar imports remained stable at around one million tonnes until domestic production costs increased rapidly in the 2010s. To address its sugar shortage, China increased imports from the international market. In 2021, sugar imports rose to 5.5 million tonnes, mainly sourced from Brazil. Most cassava

[13] China's main imported edible oil varieties include rapeseed oil, palm oil, soybean oil and sunflower oil.

product imports come from Southeast Asian countries, especially Thailand. The rise in maize prices since the mid-2000s contributed to an upward trend in China's net imports of dried cassava. However, the net import of dried cassava decreased to 262.6 million tonnes in 2021, a 68.9% increase from the 2020 level.

With decades of consecutive economic growth, China's dietary preferences shifted towards an animal product-dominant diet after the mid-2000s. This shift significantly increased the demand for fodder grains, shaping the structure of agricultural imports. Since 2009, China's dependence on imports of non-staple food crops, especially soybeans (as oilseeds) and DDGS, has generally increased. In contrast, the import patterns of wheat and sorghum have fluctuated after 2009. Wheat and sorghum, which serve as substitutes for maize in providing energy for animal fodder, have seen their use closely tied to the maize market. Their import levels are affected by changes in the production-consumption gap of maize. The higher costs associated with using wheat as a fodder grain make sorghum imports even more sensitive to fluctuations in the maize production-consumption gap. This illustrates China's external dependence on food trade to meet its fodder grain requirements, highlighting the significant impact of global agricultural dynamics on China's food security.

Classification of Imported Fodder Commodities

China's participation in the international grain trade has heavily centred on the fodder industry. In response to economic conflicts with the intentional community, particularly trade sanctions imposed by the United States, understanding the structure of China's major fodder commodity imports is crucial for assessing the country's bargaining power[14] and, consequently, its terms of trade on the global stage.

[14] In this analysis, oil meals domestically produced from imported oilseeds, such as soybean meals, are excluded from the statistical assessment of direct fodder imports.

Fodder commodities can be primarily categorised into three major types[15]: energy fodder crops, protein fodder crops and prepared fodder.[16] In China, energy fodder is commonly used in the poultry industry, whereas protein fodder is typically used in the pig industry. With the rapid growth of the animal husbandry sector, processed fodder has become increasingly popular for raising small animals. As most of China's arable land is reserved for staple food grain production to ensure self-sufficiency in food grains, the majority of the country's fodder commodity imports fall into the first two categories: energy fodder and protein fodder crops. In 2021, excluding domestically produced soybean meals used as protein fodder, imports of energy fodder constituted the largest share of China's direct fodder imports, followed by protein fodder crops.

Maize, a key component of energy fodder, is extensively used in poultry fodder in China. Until 2007, China was a net exporter of maize; however, the situation changed in 2009 when China transitioned to becoming a net importer, a shift directly linked to the increasing demand for fodder grains. This surge in demand was driven by the dietary transition of the Chinese population as the country progressed to the upper-middle-income category. Therefore, maize has become the main energy source in animal fodder. China's maize imports have shown a consistent upward trend, surging from 2.8 million tonnes in 2017 to a remarkable 28.4 million tonnes in 2021.[17]

In the category of protein fodder, soybean meal is the primary ingredient, followed by other oilseed meals, fish meal and vegetable meal, and

[15] For additional information on animal fodder, please refer to the work by Hendy, C.R.C., Ulrich Kleih, Robin Crawshaw, and M. Phillips. "Interactions between Livestock Production Systems and the Environment: Impact Domain: Concentrate Feed Demand." *FAO Consultancy report for Livestock and the Environment Study*. Rome: Food and Agriculture Organization, 1995.

[16] Energy fodder, also known as "energy feeds," is defined as low-protein concentrates with a protein content of less than 20%. Fodder containing 20% or more protein is categorised as protein fodder crops (also known as protein feeds). For more information, refer to the Food and Agriculture Organization. *Fish Feed Technology*. Rome: Food and Agriculture Organization, 1980.

[17] The consumption rate of fodder maize has been increasing much faster than that of all other food crops. As a result, maize production surpassed that of wheat in 1995 and rice in 2011, making it as the leading crop in China's agricultural production structure. By 2021, maize output had reached an impressive 272.6 million tonnes. However, total maize consumption for the same year was even higher, at approximately 288.6 million tonnes. Of this consumption, more than two-thirds was attributed for fodder maize, with the remainder used for industrial purposes.

whey powder/protein concentrates. These protein fodders are predominantly used in pig farming. While most soybean meal used in China is produced domestically, the volume of direct imports remains relatively modest. Over the past 20 years, there has been a substantial increase in China's imports of both maize and soybean as fodder crops. This growing reliance on the international commodity market for these imports has raised concerns not just domestically within China but also in the broader international community.

Table 3.2 provides a detailed breakdown of China's imports of energy and protein fodder commodities, outlining their respective shares within

Table 3.2 Classification of fodder imports by HS codes

Panel a Classification of fodder imports

	Energy fodder	Protein fodder	Prepared fodder
	(1)	(2)	(3)
Four-digit HS codes	Cassava (manioc) (0714); Barley (1003); Oats (1004); Maize (1005); Sorghum (1007); Others—residues and waste for animal feeding (2302); Brewing or distilling dregs and waste (2303).	Whey and modified whey (0404); Flour meal and pellet meat, flour meal and pellet of fish crustaceans (2301); Soybean oilcake and other solid residues (2304); Peanut oilcake and solid residue (2305); Rapeseed oilcake and solid residues, low erucic acid, oilcake, among others, from vegetable fats and oils (2306).	Preparations used in animal feeding (2309).

Panel *b* Share of energy, protein and prepared fodder in total fodder crop imports

Year	Energy fodder as % of total fodder imports	Protein fodder as % of total fodder imports	Prepared fodder as % of total fodder imports
	(4)	(5)	(6)
2016	66%	30%	4%
2017	57%	38%	5%
2021	77%	22%	1%
2022	74%	25%	1%

Note: Statistical calibre here is restricted to direct imports of fodder and fodder crops; hence, soybean meals produced domestically are not calculated in Panel b

Source: General Administration of Customs of China. *Customs Statistics*. Http://stats.customs.gov.cn/indexEn. Accessed January 15, 2024

each sub-category for the years 2016–2017 and 2021–2022. This comparative analysis examines China's fodder commodity trade structure before and after the onset of the Sino-US trade war. The selected sub-categories (Table 3.2, Panel a) are listed under the four-digit Harmonised System (HS) codes, following the World Bank's World Integrated Trade Solution guidelines.[18] The statistical calibre is specifically restricted to the direct imports of fodder grains, thereby excluding domestically processed soybean meals made from imported soybeans.

When excluding domestically produced soybean meals, energy fodder constituted the majority of China's direct fodder imports, accounting for 74–77% in 2021–2022. This represents a significant increase from the 57–66% recorded in 2016–2017 (Table 3.2, Panel b). In contrast, the imports of protein fodder commodities in China declined from 30–38% in 2016–2017 to 22–25% in 2021–2022.

In energy fodder crops, maize has been widely used as a key ingredient in poultry farming. China became a net importer of maize since 2009, after being a net exporter until 2007. This shift aligns with a period of accelerated demand for fodder grains. Since the mid-2000s, maize has progressively become the main energy source for animal fodder. The volume of China's recent maize imports has fluctuated, influenced by local output and consumption levels. In 2021, maize imports reached 28.4 million tonnes,[19] equivalent to US$8.0 billion or 39.6% of the total energy fodder imports for the year (Table 3.3, Panel a, Column 3). Substitutes for maize in energy fodder have also experienced fluctuations. For example, sorghum imports in China increased from 15.0% (Column 3) to 36.0% (Column 4) of the total energy fodder imports in 2021–2022, primarily due to the spike in maize prices in 2021. Another substitute, DDGS, saw significant changes. As maize imports rose, DDGS imports declined from a peak of 6.8 million tonnes[20] in 2015 to approximately 83.4 thousand

[18] World Bank. *World Integrated Trade Solution.* Https://wits.worldbank.org. Accessed January 15, 2024.

[19] Ministry of Agriculture and Rural Affairs of China. "*Situations on China's Import and Export of Agricultural Products from January to December 2022 (2022 Nian 1–12 yue woguo nongchanpin jin chukou qingkuang).*" Published January 18, 2023. Http://www.moa.gov.cn/ztzl/nybrl/rlxx/202301/t20230128_6419275.htm. Accessed January 15, 2024.

[20] Ministry of Agriculture and Rural Affairs of China. "*Data on China's Import and Export of Agricultural Products from January to December 2015 (2015 Nian 1–12 yue woguo nongchanpin jinchukou shuju).*" Published February 01, 2016. Http://www.moa.gov.cn/ztzl/nybrl/rlxx/201602/t20160202_5006675.htm. Accessed January 15, 2024.

Table 3.3 Structure of China's protein and energy fodder imports

Panel a Energy fodder varieties	*Share in total import of energy fodder*			
	2016	*2017*	*2021*	*2022*
	(1)	*(2)*	*(3)*	*(4)*
Cassava (0714)	26%	28%	8%	20%
Barley (1003)	22%	35%	18%	20%
Oats (1004)	1%	2%	18%	1%
Sorghum (1007)	25%	19%	15%	36%
Brewing or distilling dregs and waste, DDGS (2303)	13%	1%	0.5%	0.3%
Other energy fodder (2302, 2303)	2%	3%	2%	6%
Panel b Protein fodder varieties	*Share in total import of protein fodder*			
	2016	*2017*	*2021*	*2022*
	(5)	*(6)*	*(7)*	*(8)*
Whey and modified whey (0404)[a]	19%	20%	17%	9%
Flour, meal and pellet of fish; and of meat (2301)	71%	68%	51%	23%
Soybean oilcake and solid residues (2304)	1%	1%	1%	1%
Peanut oilcake and solid residues (2305)	1%	1%	0.3%	2%
Rapeseed oilcake, oilcake from vegetable fats (2306)	8%	10%	18%	34%

Source: General Administration of Customs of China. *Customs Statistics*. Http://stats.customs.gov.cn/indexEn. Accessed January 15, 2024

[a]Whey and modified whey, whether or not concentrated or containing added sugar or other sweetening matter

tonnes in 2022, representing only 0.3% of all energy fodder imports for the year (Column 4).[21]

Within the protein fodder category (Table 3.3, Panel b), soybean meal is the main ingredient, followed closely by other oilseed meals, fish meal and vegetable meal, which are predominantly used in pig farming. Most soybean meal consumed in China is produced domestically, resulting in a consistently low volume of direct imports, which accounts for only 1% of the total protein fodder imports. In addition to soybean meal, protein

[21] Since DDGS can partially substitute both energy and protein fodder, its imports drew the attention of the Chinese government. This led to the initiation of an anti-dumping investigation into DDGS imports from the United States as early as the end of 2010. The findings of the investigation resulted in DDGS being placed under regular monitoring and incorporated into China's bulk agricultural commodity reporting system.

fodder supplements include fish meals, meat meals and whey powder/ protein concentrates. In 2021, fish and meat meals represented 50.9% of China's protein fodder import value, with whey powder contributing 17.0% (Column 7). However, this distribution changed in 2022, with fish meals accounting for 22.9% and whey powder for 9.5% of the import value (Column 8).

The major sources of China's energy fodder include the United States, Ukraine, Australia and Thailand (Table 3.4). In contrast, protein fodder mainly originates from Peru, Canada and the United States. Despite a substantial decrease in protein fodder imports (Table 3.2) and efforts to diversify sources beyond the United States to reduce import dependence, the United States remains a leading exporter to China in most years following the onset of the Sino-US trade war. Additionally, when considering imports of soybeans from the United States and Brazil, which are subsequently processed domestically into soybean meals for protein fodder, the United States continues to be the most significant exporter of fodder commodities to China among all the major exporters listed in Table 3.4.

Table 3.4 China's major trade partners of fodder imports

	Exporters, % share in each category			
	2016	*2017*	*2021*	*2022*
	(1)	(2)	(3)	(4)
Energy forage crops	①The United States 35%	①Australia 28%	①The United States 39%	①The United States 23%
	②Thailand 22%	②Thailand 23%	②Ukraine 16%	②Thailand 18%
	③Australia 17%	③The United States 23%	③Thailand 7%	③Ukraine 17%
Protein forage crops	①Peru 29%	①Peru 36%	①Peru 26%	①Canada 24%
	②The United States 19%	②The United States 16%	②Ukraine 13%	②Ukraine 19%
	③Vietnam 7%	③Canada 8%	③The United States 11%	③Vietnam 6%
Prepared fodder	①The United States 28%	①The United States 29%	①Thailand 49%	①Thailand 50%
	②France 6%	②Netherlands 13%	②Japan 15%	②Japan 15%
	③Netherlands 6%	③Thailand 9%	③Germany 9%	③Italy 14%

Source: General Administration of Customs of China. *Customs Statistics*. Http://stats.customs.gov.cn/indexEn. Accessed January 15, 2024

Fodder Commodity Imports and Dependence

Import Dependence by Product Varieties

At the outset of the Sino-US trade war, China was importing approximately US$24 billion annually in agricultural and related goods from the United States.[22] This figure steadily increased to US$35.5 billion[23] in 2022, accounting for 10.6% of China's total agricultural product imports for that year. Among these imports, fodder commodities took the largest share, positioning them at the forefront of trade and economic tensions between the United States and China, with soybeans and maize being prime examples. Understanding the significance of these major imported fodder commodities is crucial for comprehending the influence of economic disputes on agriculture and related industries in China.

- **Maize:** The majority of maize used for poultry fodder in China has been domestically cultivated,[24] showing the country's long-standing policy support for maize. Before the termination of the temporary storage policy for maize in April 2016,[25] the Chinese government purchased maize to prevent domestic prices from falling below the protection price. This policy made China's domestic maize more expensive than international market prices, thereby encouraging imports.[26] However, after the cancellation of the maize temporary storage policy in 2016, a large quantity of stored maize was released

[22] Li, Minghao, Wendong Zhang, and Hart Chad. "Lessons from Previous U.S.-China Trade Disputes." *Iowa State University, Center for Agricultural and Rural Development Agricultural Policy Review*. Https://www.card.iastate.edu/ag_policy_review/article/?a=80. Accessed January 15, 2024.

[23] Office of Technology Evaluation, Department of Commerce, Bureau of Industry and Security of the United States. "2022. U.S. Trade with China." Published 2022. Https://www.bis.doc.gov/index.php/country-papers/3268-2022-statistical-analysis-of-u-s-trade-with-china/file. Accessed January 15, 2024.

[24] As the consumption of fodder maize has grown much faster than all other food crops, maize output overtook that of both rice and wheat in 2011, making it the leading crop in China.

[25] For details, refer to National Food and Strategic Reserves Administration. "*Notice on Issues Related to the Procurement of National Maize Temporary Storage in Northeast China in 2015 (Guanyu 2015 nian dongbei diqu guojia linshi cunchu yumi shougou youguan wenti de tongzhi).*" Published in September 18, 2015. Http://www.lswz.gov.cn/html/zcfb/2018-06/12/content_216632.shtml. Accessed January 15, 2024.

[26] However, the importation of maize continued to be restricted by the tariff-rate quota.

into the market, resulting in increased consumption of domestic maize. Fodder industries, which had previously relied on imports of substitutes like sorghum—unrestricted by import quota—returned to domestic maize following the policy change. As a result, imports of maize and its major substitutes in energy fodder declined since 2017.[27] Despite a quick reduction in maize stockpiles from their peak in 2016 and maintaining steady maize production, China's domestic supply has remained insufficient to meet domestic demand. The country has continued to import significant quantities of maize to address the production-consumption gap. With the depletion of domestic maize stock and limited availability of farmland for reallocating to fodder maize and/or soybean cultivation, maize imports have, as expected, resumed an upward trend, which has persisted (Fig. 3.2).

In 2021, eight countries and regions dominated global maize production in 2021, collectively contributing to nearly 80% of the total global maize output.[28] China's maize imports in 2021 accounted for only 3.6% of global maize exports, indicating a relatively low level of dependence on the United States for maize.[29]

As alternatives to maize, wheat, sorghum and DDGS are viable energy sources. While wheat can serve as a substitute for maize in poultry fodder, its higher cost raises concerns about its impact on the domestic food supply and overall food security. In contrast, sorghum and DDGS offer a cost advantage, making their imports more sensitive to fluctuations in maize supply.[30] Consequently, China's regula-

[27] In 2017, China's imported 2.8 million tonnes of maize. By 2022, this figure increased to 20.6 million tonnes, highlighting a significant growth in maize imports. As of 2022, the primary sources of maize (excluding seed maize) imported into China were the United States and Ukraine.

[28] Sorted in descending order based on their respective shares, the top maize-producing countries in 2021 were the United States (32%), China (22%), Brazil (10%), the European Union (6%), Argentina (4%), Ukraine (4%), India (3%) and Mexico (2%).

[29] While the sown area and production of maize show minor fluctuations globally, there are significant disparities among countries. In particular, Ukraine and Russia have experienced the most rapid expansions in their maize-sown areas. Since 2015, Ukraine has surpassed the United States as the leading source of maize imports to China. This change occurred after China rejected maize shipments from the United States due to the detection of a genetically modified strain not approved for import.

[30] For example, following the abolition of China's temporary maize storage policy in 2016, sorghum imports dropped by 37.9%. Further details can be found in the report by the

tions on maize imports may not necessarily encourage the use of domestic wheat; instead, they could lead to increased reliance on imported sorghum and DDGS. This partly explains why China previously initiated anti-dumping investigations into imports of both sorghum and DDGS from the United States, which is the most significant supplier of these commodities to the Chinese market.

- **Soybean and Soybean Meal:** Soybean meal, a by-product of soybean crushing, holds the largest share in China's domestic consumption of protein fodder.[31] While alternatives such as vegetable meals, some other oilseed meals (e.g. peanut meal) and DDGS are available, their production levels limit their substitutive effect. The ongoing high demand for protein fodder has consistently driven soybean consumption. To encourage soybean cultivation, the Chinese government shifted from a target price-based direct subsidy for soybean planting to a market-oriented approach, supplemented by direct subsidies.[32] This adjustment provided additional support for farmers engaged in soybean cultivation.[33] Regions such as Anhui, Inner Mongolia and the Northeast Provinces have prioritised soybean production. Notably, Heilongjiang, the leading soybean-producing province, reported approximately 74.0 million mu (equivalent to 29.9 million hectares) of soybean sown area in 2022, accounting for 48.9% of the total soybean sown area in China for the year.[34] All

Ministry of Agriculture and Rural Affairs of China. "*Situations on China's Import and Export of Agricultural Products from January to December 2016 (2016 Nian 1–12 yue woguo nongchanpin jinchukou qingkuang).*" Published February 04, 2017. Http://www.moa.gov.cn/ztzl/nybrl/rlxx/201702/t20170207_5469872.htm. Accessed January 15, 2024.

[31] Soybean meal accounts for approximately three-quarters of China's domestic consumption of protein fodder.

[32] Central Committee of the CCP. "*Document No. 1 of 2022. Opinions of the Central Committee of the Communist Party of China and the State Council on the Key Works to Comprehensively Promote Rural Revitalization in 2022 (Zhonggong zhongyang, guowuyuan guanyu zuohao 2023 nian quanmian tuijin xiangcun zhenxing zhongdian gongzuo de yijian).*" Beijing: The Central Committee of the CCP and the State Council of China Document, January 4, 2022.

[33] As a result, in 2022, China's domestic soybean-sown area increased by approximately 21.7% compared to the previous year, reaching its highest level since 1958.

[34] Heilongjiang Daily. "*Two Firsts in the Country! Sown Area and Total Output of Soybean in Heilongjiang Have Hit Historical Record Highs (Liang xiang quqnguo di yi! Heilongjiang dadou bozhong mianji, zong chanliang jun chuang lishi zuigao jilu).*" Published December 16, 2022. Https://www.hlj.gov.cn/hlj/c107856/202212/c00_31502977.shtml. Accessed January 15, 2024.

these efforts brought China a substantial soybean harvest of 20.3 million tonnes in 2022.

Nevertheless, China's increasing demand for soybean continues to outpace domestic production, leading to a heavy reliance on imports.[35] The volume of soybean imports remained consistently high at 91.1 million tonnes in 2021 and 96.5 million tonnes in 2022. This rapid growth in soybean imports has resulted in high accumulations of soybean meal inventories in China, compelling some crushing plants to temporarily halt operations to manage the stockpile. Therefore, while imports of soybeans and soybean meal are expected to continue growing, high domestic stocks and uncertainties in economic relations with the United States may moderate China's needs for imported soybeans.

- **DDGS:** DDGS have served as a viable alternative for both energy and protein fodder. Scientific estimates suggest that substituting DDGS for up to 20% of maize and soybean meals traditionally used in animal fodder could reduce costs.[36] Despite China being one of the largest maize producers and DDGS being a co-product of dry-milled ethanol production from a mix of grains, mainly maize, reports indicate that DDGS co-product from the United States is superior in quality and consistency. This distinction is largely due to the prevalence of mycotoxins (e.g. aflatoxin) in domestically produced DDGS in China.

The import tariff rate for DDGS has traditionally been lower than that for maize. As a result, beginning in the late 2000s, China significantly increased its DDGS imports, mainly from the United States. The rise in import volume was driven by the increasing costs of other fodder ingredients, which led China's livestock industry to seek more cost-effective alternatives.[37] By 2010, China's imports of

[35] This increase is due not only to the increasing domestic demand for edible oil but also, more significantly, to the expanding need for soybean meal in China's fast-growing swine industry.

[36] Fabiosa, Jacinto F. "Distillers Dried Grain Product Innovation and Its Impact on Adoption, Inclusion, Substitution and displacement Rates in a Finishing Hog Ration." *Working Paper 08-WP478* Centre for Agricultural and Rural Development, Iowa State University, 2008.

[37] Jewison, Michael, and Fred Gale. "China's Market for Distillers Dried Grains and the Key Influences on Its Longer Run Potential." *Feed Outlook No. FDS-12G-01*. United States Department of Agriculture, 2012.

American DDGS had reached 2.5 million tonnes, surpassing both Mexico and Canada, and making China the largest importer of the United States' DDGS.[38] However, this trend faced a downturn in 2021 when China launched an anti-dumping investigation into DDGS from the United States, imposing restrictions on imports from this source.

Following the abandonment of the anti-dumping investigation by China's Commerce Ministry, DDGS imports experienced a resurgence. In 2014 and 2015, there was a substantial surge in DDGS imports, partly due to China's inspection and quarantine authorities rejecting shipments of the United States' maize because of the detection of an unapproved genetically modified variety. However, the situation was reversed when the Chinese government imposed anti-dumping tariffs on United States' DDGS of up to 53.7%, along with an additional retaliatory tariff rate of 25% during the trade war (Table 3.2 under HS code 2303). These measures led to a shift towards substituting imports with sorghum and barley while also intensifying efforts to increase domestic maize production.

Import Dependence by Originating Countries

Comparing different food trade varieties can be challenging, as available trade volume data may not fully capture the significance of each exporting country's contributions. Therefore, the specific share of bilateral food imports that China receives from each country remains unclear. To better understand China's food import dependence, the concept of "virtual land" is used, following the method of "ghost acreage" developed by economic historians.[39]

[38] The United States is the biggest exporter of DDGS. In 1996, its export volume was 0.5 million tonnes, which quickly increased to 9.0 million tonnes in 2010, reflecting an impressive annual growth rate of 32%. Before the early 2000s, European countries such as Ireland, the United Kingdom and Spain were among the major importers of DDGS from the United States. However, in 2006, Mexico surpassed the European Union to become the leading importer of DDGS from the United States, only to be overtaken by China in 2010.

[39] For a detailed discussion on the "ghost acreage" and resources China utilised to support domestic industrial growth, please refer to the section titled "*Economic Growth Dependent on 'Ghost Resources'*" in Chap. 4.

Virtual land calculations offer a unique perspective, estimating that China utilised a total of 86.4 million hectares of overseas virtual farmland in 2021, far exceeding China's current "red line" of 1.8 billion mu (about 120 million hectares). Figure 3.3 visually illustrates China's import dependence on its partner countries based on these farmland utilisation estimates.

In 2021, China imports of virtual farmland were most intense from Brazil, the United States, Argentina, followed by Canada, New Zealand, Ukraine and Australia, listed in descending order of intensity.

- **Brazil**: It stood as China's top food exporter in 2021, accounting for nearly 41.2% of the world's food exports to China, as per the virtual land-based calculation system. The total net farmland used in Brazil amounted to 35.6 million hectares, with soybeans taking the largest share at 58.2 million tonnes, followed by sugar.
- **The United States:** Following Brazil, the United States ranked the second-largest food supplier to China in 2021, accounting for 27.7% of China's total virtual farmland use abroad. The primary import from the United States was soybeans, amounting to 32.3 million tonnes or 33.5% of China's total soybean imports for the year. Maize imports from the United States also surged to 28.4 million tonnes.

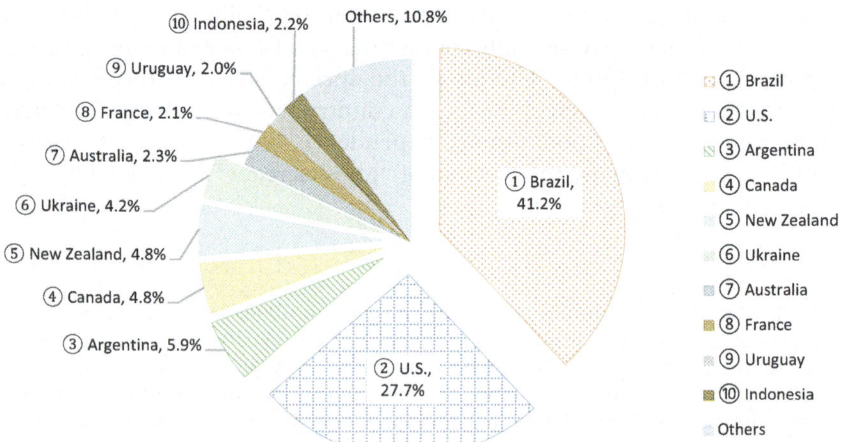

Fig. 3.3 Distribution of "farmland import" by products and country of origins, 2021 level

Sorghum imports followed, with China importing 4.3 million tonnes from the United States out of a sum of 9.4 million tonnes for the year. Despite the diverse nature of China's virtual land use in the United States, the focus remained on fodder crops. The US-China trade in maize and sorghum constituted 15.3% and 45.2% of China's total maize and sorghum trade, respectively, in 2021. Thus, China's reliance on agricultural products from the United States has been predominantly fodder-oriented, rather than dependent on a single product.

- **Argentina and Canada:** Following Brazil and the United States, Argentina and Canada, respectively, represent 5.9% and 4.8% of China's total overseas virtual land use. In 2021, Argentina's exports to China were primarily soybeans (3.7 million tonnes), soybean oil (0.5 million tonnes) and sorghum (0.4 million tonnes). Canada's exports to China were more diversified, including rapeseed (2.4 million tonnes) and rapeseed oil (0.9 million tonnes), wheat (2.3 million tonnes) and barley (2.0 million tonnes). Unlike the import pattern from Brazil and the United States, which focused mainly on fodder crops, Argentina and Canada's trade with China was predominantly centred on oilseeds (i.e. soybeans and rapeseeds) and edible oils (i.e. soybean oil and rapeseed oil), indicating a partially food-oriented land use pattern.
- **New Zealand, Ukraine and Australia:** Beyond the top four countries, China's overseas virtual land use in New Zealand (4.8%), Ukraine (4.2%) and Australia (2.3%)—ranked fifth to seventh—totalled 9.8 million hectares, or 11.3% of the total overseas virtual land use by the Chinese. In 2021, China's net import from New Zealand was primarily milk products. Imports from Ukraine and Australia, along with France (ranking eighth), were mainly maize, wheat and barley.

The most recent data from the Ministry of Land and Resources of China, as of 2022, shows that the country had about 127.6 million hectares of farmland.[40] In 2021, the overseas virtual farmland use, equivalent

[40] Ministry of Land and Resources of China. *2022 China Land Resource Bulletin (2022 Nian zhongguo ziran ziyuan tongji gongbao)*. Published April 2023. Https://www.mnr.gov.cn/sj/tjgb/202304/P020230412557301980490.pdf. Accessed January 15, 2024.

to China's food imports, amounted to 86.4 million hectares. This constitutes roughly 67.7% of the total farmland resources in China. Among China's trading partners, virtual farmland exports from Brazil and the United States constituted 27.9% and 18.7%, respectively, of China's domestic farmland availability. Additionally, Argentina's contribution to China's food trade constituted approximately 4.0% of China's domestic farmland availability.

Among all agricultural products imported by China, soybeans have taken the largest share, a trend propelled by the country's extensive urbanisation programme. This urbanisation has raised the demand for both edible oil and animal protein. Notably, Soybeans are versatile: they can be crushed to produce edible oil or used as fodder meal for the livestock industry. This observation aligns with earlier analyses based on import volumes, which suggests that China's agricultural imports are heavily concentrated on a few land-intensive, non-staple food crops, which are used both directly and indirectly as fodder grain.

China's top trading partners for fodder grain—namely Brazil, the United States and Argentina—dominate the market share. However, compared to Brazil and Argentina, China's dependence on food product imports is significantly more skewed towards the United States.

Food Products as Targets in Sino-US Trade Conflicts

In 2018–2019, escalating trade tensions between China and the United States spurred widespread discussions about their economic relationship. The United States initiated several rounds of tariffs on Chinese imports, making China to respond with comparable duties on American exports. For example, in April 2018, China levied a substantial tariff of about 179% on the United States' sorghum.[41] Later, the United States announced an additional 25% tariff on Chinese imports totalling US$200 billion.[42] In

[41] Ministry of Commerce of China. "*Announcement No. 38 of 2018 from the Ministry of Commerce (Zhonghua renmin gongheguo shangwu bu gonggao 2018 nian di 38 hao).*" Http://www.mofcom.gov.cn/article/b/g/201805/20180502744597.shtml. Accessed January 15, 2024.

[42] Office of the United States Trade Representative. 2018. "*Statement by U.S. Trade Representative Robert Lighthizer on Section 301 Action.*" Https://ustr.gov/about-us/policy-offices/press-office/press-releases/2018/july/statement-us-trade-representative. Accessed January 15, 2024.

response, the Chinese government imposed tariffs on US$60 billion worth of American exports, with a significant portion targeting agricultural products (Table 3.5).[43]

Given that agricultural commodities constitute a large portion of China's imports from the United States, they have become a primary focus of China's retaliatory tariffs. This strategy not only impacted the American farming sector but also had considerable repercussions for China itself. China's leading sources of agricultural imports are Brazil and the United States. Brazil has been a significant supplier of oilseeds (i.e. soybean) and sugar to China, while the United States has not only provided a substantial share of oilseeds but also been a major source of various fodder imports (i.e. maize, sorghum and DDGS).

The tensions in the economic relationship between the United States and China may take time to resolve, and the final impact on the agricultural sectors of both countries remains uncertain. Setting aside political and ideological differences, the economic effects of the trade conflict are largely based on each country's import substitution and dependence on imported products. Comparatively, China, which houses 22% of the global population, possesses only 7% of the world's total arable land area. The country has primarily exported labour-intensive industrial goods globally, especially to the United States, while the United States has been a major supplier of farmland-intensive agricultural products to China. These contrasts in population size, availability of arable land and trade dynamics highlight the complexity of the economic interdependence between China and the United States, complicating China's stance in the trade tensions.

A small change on a large base may not have the same significance as a large change on a small base. This principle is particularly relevant in the context of the fodder commodity trade between the United States and China, where changes tend to have a more significant impact on China than on the United States. The Chinese husbandry industry's heavy dependence on fodder products imported from the United States makes

[43] Customs Tariff Commission of the State Council. "*Announcement of the Customs Tariff Commission of the State Council on Imposing Additional Tariffs on Certain Imports Originating in the United States (Second Group) (Guowuyuan guanshui shuize weiyuanhui guanyu dui yuan chan yu meiguo de bufen jinkou shangpin [di er pi] jia zheng guanshui de gonggao)*." Published August 03, 2018. Https://www.gov.cn/xinwen/2018-08/03/content_5311619.htm. Accessed January 15, 2024.

Table 3.5 Selected China's imports of agricultural products from the United States subject to additional tariffs in 2018

Four-digit HS code	*Article information*	*Additional tariff*
1201	Yellow soya beans, whether or not broken, other than for seed	25%
	Black soya beans, whether or not broken, other than for seed	25%
1102	Maize (corn) flour	25%
2303	Brewing or distilling dregs and waste	25%
0201	Meat of bovine animals, carcasses and half carcasses, fresh or chilled	25%
0203	Hams, shoulders and cuts of wild swine, with bone in, fresh or chilled	25%
0207	Chicken cut, with bone, fresh or chilled	25%
	Meat of ducks, not cut in pieces, fresh or chilled	25%
1006	Husked (brown) rice, long grain	25%
0714	Chilled or frozen sweet potatoes (whether or not sliced or in the form of pellets)	20%
1601	Sausages and similar products, with a natural casing	20%
0710	Potatoes (uncooked or cooked by steaming or boiling in water), frozen	10%
	Sweet corn, (uncooked or cooked by steaming or boiling in water), frozen	10%
	Vegetables, not elsewhere specified or included (uncooked or cooked by steaming or boiling in water), frozen	10%
2301	Flours and meals of fish, of a kind used in animal feeding	25%

Source: Customs Tariff Commission of the State Council. "*Announcement of the Customs Tariff Commission of the State Council on Imposing Additional Tariffs on USD50 Billion Imports of Products Originating in the United States (Guowuyuan guanshui shuize weiyuanhui guanyu dui yuan chan yu meiguo 500 yi meiyuan jinkou shangpin jia zheng guanshui de gonggao)*." Https://www.gov.cn/xinwen/2018-06/16/content_5299069.htm. Accessed February 15, 2024; Customs Tariff Commission of the State Council. "*Announcement of the Customs Tariff Commission of the State Council on Imposing Additional Tariffs on Certain Imports Originating in the United States (Second Group) (Guowuyuan guanshui shuize weiyuanhui guanyu dui yuan chan yu meiguo de bufen jinkou shangpin [di er pi] jia zheng guanshui de gonggao)*." Published August 03, 2018. Https://www.gov.cn/xinwen/2018-08/03/content_5311619.htm. Accessed January 15, 2024; Customs Tariff Commission of the State Council. "*Announcement of the Customs Tariff Commission of the State Council on Imposing Additional Tariffs on Approximately USD16 Billion Imports of Products Originating in the United States (Guowuyuan guanshui shuize weiyuanhui guanyu dui yuan chan yu meiguo yue 160 yi meiyuan jinkou shangpin jia zheng guanshui de gonggao)*." Https://www.gov.cn/xinwen/2018-08/08/content_5312624.htm. Accessed February 15, 2024; Ministry of Commerce of China. "*Announcement on Imposing Additional Tariff on Several Imports of Products Originating in the United States (Guanyu dui yuan chan yu meiguo de bufen jinkou shangpin jia zheng guanshui de gonggao)*." Published April 04, 2018. Http://www.mofcom.gov.cn/article/ae/ai/201804/20180402728484.shtml. Accessed January 15, 2024

China more vulnerable to changes in trade policies.[44] When comparing protein fodder to energy fodder, the latter may be less affected by the deteriorating bilateral economic relations. China, as one of the world's leading maize producers, has the capacity to partially offset the effects of potential disruptions in protein fodder imports by relying on its domestic maize production. Additionally, despite China's imposition of retaliatory tariffs on sorghum—as substitute to maize—the country still has other options in the international maize market. This availability of alternatives could help soften the blow of bilateral tensions on the use of energy fodder, thereby minimising potential disruptions.

China's imposition of anti-dumping duties on American DDGS and retaliatory tariff on soybeans has immediately impacted the protein fodder market. The ongoing economic tensions may lead to further consequences, depending on whether domestic soybean meal stockpiles can be sustained until China can increase its domestic soybean cultivation to meet domestic needs, similar to the success observed in its Northeastern Provinces.

In terms of meat consumption, the 2018–2019 outbreak of African Swine Fever prompted a shift in domestic consumption preferences towards poultry. Faced with rising costs of protein fodder, the domestic animal industry has increased the supply of poultry to partially compensate for the reduced pork consumption during this dietary transition. As a result, China's livestock and husbandry industries are expected to adjust their fodder commodity imports, seeking a balance between protein and energy fodder varieties in response to these changing dynamics.

By the end of 2021, China's agricultural import-equivalent land use had increased to 67.7% of the total available farmland within the country. Despite its awareness of the growing reliance on overseas food imports, the Chinese government may struggle to the substantial domestic demand for fodder grains unless there is a reversal in the population's dietary patterns. Therefore, the country's dependence on imported food is expected to remain high.

China's current agricultural imports mainly come from Brazil and the United States. The range of agricultural and related products imported from Brazil is relatively straightforward, focusing mainly on oilseeds and food-related items such as sugar, as well as various types of fodder. In

[44] As the market evolves, other exporters, such as Brazil, are well-positioned to capture a larger share of China's agricultural imports.

contrast, the United States provides the majority of China's imports of sorghum and DDGS, along with significant quantities of soybean and maize. Given that soybeans are processed into meal for use as protein fodder, the United States maintains its position as China's leading supplier of fodder commodities.

Unlike imports of manufacturing products, which often hinge on the trade partner's comparative advantage of lower factor costs, food imports highlight a domestic scarcity of per capita land resources. Despite China's emergence as the largest manufacturer in the world and the significant expansion of its industrial sector's global influence, the country remains vulnerable due to its dependence on imported fodder commodities. This dependence could influence the general terms and conditions of trade, adding complexity to China's economic environment. The growing demand for fodder grains, combined with the limited land resources reserved for staple crop farming, has intensified China's dependence on international trade and its susceptibility to external economic and political factors. This, in turn, has led to non-agricultural issues with exporting countries. All these dynamics have highlighted a new food problem into sharp focus: the delicate balance between domestic food self-sufficiency and the trade in food commodities. Addressing this challenge will not only affect China's agricultural performance but also influence the country's trajectory of economic growth.

References

Central Committee of the CCP. "*Document No. 1 of 2022. Opinions of the Central Committee of the Communist Party of China and the State Council on the Key Works to Comprehensively Promote Rural Revitalization in 2022 (Zhonggong zhongyang, guowuyuan guanyu zuohao 2023 nian quanmian tuijin xiangcun zhenxing zhongdian gongzuo de yijian).*" Beijing: Central Committee of the CCP and the State Council of China, January 4, 2022.

Customs Tariff Commission of the State Council. "*Announcement of the Customs Tariff Commission of the State Council on Imposing Additional Tariffs on Certain Imports Originating in the United States (Second Group) (Guowuyuan guanshui shuize weiyuanhui guanyu dui yuan chan yu meiguo de bufen jinkou shangpin [di er pi] jia zheng guanshui de gonggao).*" Published August 03 2018. Https://www.gov.cn/xinwen/2018-08/03/content_5311619.htm. Accessed January 15, 2024a.

Customs Tariff Commission of the State Council. "*Announcement of the Customs Tariff Commission of the State Council on Imposing Additional Tariffs on USD50 Billion Imports of Products Originating in the United States (Guowuyuan guanshui shuize weiyuanhui guanyu dui yuan chan yu meiguo 500 yi meiyuan jinkou shangpin jia zheng guanshui de gonggao).*" Https://www.gov.cn/xinwen/2018-06/16/content_5299069.htm. Accessed February 15, 2024b.

Customs Tariff Commission of the State Council. "*Announcement of the Customs Tariff Commission of the State Council on Imposing Additional Tariffs on Approximately USD16 Billion Imports of Products Originating in the United States (Guowuyuan guanshui shuize weiyuanhui guanyu dui yuan chan yu meiguo yue 160 yi meiyuan jinkou shangpin jia zheng guanshui de gonggao).*" Https://www.gov.cn/xinwen/2018-08/08/content_5312624.htm. Accessed February 15, 2024c.

Economic Daily. 2022. "Fodder Grain Supply Affects National Food Security (Siliao liang gongji guanhu guojia liangshi anquan)." Published on 7 July 2023. Http://paper.ce.cn/pad/content/202307/07/content_277029.html. Accessed January 15, 2024.

Fabiosa, Jacinto F. "Distillers Dried Grain Product Innovation and Its Impact on Adoption, Inclusion, Substitution and Displacement Rates in a Finishing Hog Ration." *Working Paper 08-WP478* Centre for Agricultural and Rural Development, Iowa State University, 2008.

Food and Agriculture Organisation of the United Nations. *FAOSTAT, Crops and Livestock Products.* Https://www.fao.org/faostat/en/#data/QCL. Accessed January 15, 2024.

Food and Agriculture Organization. *Fish Feed Technology.* Rome: Food and Agriculture Organization, 1980.

General Administration of Customs of China. *Customs Statistics.* Http://stats.customs.gov.cn/indexEn. Accessed January 15, 2024.

Guangming Daily. "Promoting the 'Three Transformations' to Build a New Development Structure of National Food Security (Tuidong 'san ge zhuanbian' goujian guojia liangshi anquan fazhan xin de geju)." Published on 11 May 2022. Https://epaper.gmw.cn/gmrb/html/2022-05/11/nw.D110000gmrb_20220511_1-06.htm. Accessed January 15, 2024.

Heilongjiang Daily. "*Two Firsts in the Country! Sown Area and Total Output of Soybean in Heilongjiang Have Hit Historical Record Highs (Liang xiang quqnguo di yi! Heilongjiang dadou bozhong mianji, zong chanliang jun chuang lishi zuigao jilu).*" Published December 16, 2022. Https://www.hlj.gov.cn/hlj/c107856/202212/c00_31502977.shtml. Accessed January 15, 2024.

Hendy, C.R.C., Ulrich Kleih, Robin Crawshaw, and M. Phillips. "Interactions between Livestock Production Systems and the Environment: Impact Domain: Concentrate Feed Demand." *FAO Consultancy report for Livestock and the Environment Study.* Rome: Food and Agriculture Organization, 1995.

Jewison, Michael, and Fred Gale. "China's Market for Distillers Dried Grains and the Key Influences on Its Longer Run Potential". *Feed Outlook No. FDS-12G-01*. United States Department of Agriculture, 2012.

Li, Minghao, Wendong Zhang, and Hart Chad. "Lessons from Previous U.S.-China Trade Disputes." *Iowa State University, Center for Agricultural and Rural Development Agricultural Policy Review.* Https://www.card.iastate.edu/ag_policy_review/article/?a=80. Accessed January 15, 2024.

Macrotrends. *Corn Prices—59 Year Historical Chart.* Https://www.macrotrends.net/2532/corn-prices-historical-chart-data. Accessed January 15, 2024.

Ministry of Agriculture and Rural Affairs of China. "*China's Import and Export of Agricultural Products in 2021 (2021 Nian woguo nongchanpin jinchukou).*" Published January 18 2023. Http://www.moa.gov.cn/ztzl/nybrl/rlxx/202201/t20220127_6387781.htm. Accessed January 15, 2024a.

Ministry of Agriculture and Rural Affairs of China. "*Data on China's Import and Export of Agricultural Products from January to December 2015 (2015 Nian 1–12 yue woguo nongchanpin jinchukou shuju).*" Published February 01, 2016. Http://www.moa.gov.cn/ztzl/nybrl/rlxx/201602/t20160202_5006675.htm. Accessed January 15, 2024b.

Ministry of Agriculture and Rural Affairs of China. "*Situations on China's Import and Export of Agricultural Products from January to December 2022 (2022 Nian 1–12 yue woguo nongchanpin jin chukou qingkuang).*" Published January 18 2023. Http://www.moa.gov.cn/ztzl/nybrl/rlxx/202301/t20230128_6419275.htm. Accessed January 15, 2024c.

Ministry of Agriculture and Rural Affairs of China. "*Situations on China's Import and Export of Agricultural Products from January to December 2016 (2016 Nian 1–12 yue woguo nongchanpin jinchukou qingkuang).*" Published February 04, 2017. Http://www.moa.gov.cn/ztzl/nybrl/rlxx/201702/t20170207_5469872.htm. Accessed January 15, 2024d.

Ministry of Agriculture and Rural Affairs of China. *Circular of the Ministry of Agriculture and Rural Affairs on Issuing the "Measures of Managing Special Fund for Protecting Arable Land Quality" (Nongyebu guanyu yinfa "gengdi zhiliang baohu zhuanxiang zijin guanli banfa" de tongzhi)*. Beijing: Ministry of Agriculture and Rural Affairs of China, January 15, 2018.

Ministry of Agriculture of China. "*China's Import and Export of Agricultural Products in 2021 (2021 Nian woguo nongchanpin jin chukou qingkuang).*" Published January 27, 2022. Http://www.moa.gov.cn/ztzl/nybrl/rlxx/202201/t20220127_6387781.htm. Accessed January 15, 2024.

Ministry of Commerce of China. "*Announcement No. 38 of 2018 from the Ministry of Commerce (Zhonghua renmin gongheguo shangwu bu gonggao 2018 nian di 38 hao).*" Http://www.mofcom.gov.cn/article/b/g/201805/20180502744597.shtml. Accessed January 15, 2024a.

Ministry of Commerce of China. "*Announcement on Imposing Additional Tariff on Several Imports of Products Originating in the United States (Guanyu dui yuan chan yu meiguo de bufen jinkou shangpin jia zheng guanshui de gonggao).*" Published April 04, 2018. Http://www.mofcom.gov.cn/article/ae/ai/201804/20180402728484.shtml. Accessed January 15, 2024b.

Ministry of Land and Resources of China. *2022 China Land Resource Bulletin (2022 Nian zhongguo ziran ziyuan tongji gongbao).* Published April 2023. Https://www.mnr.gov.cn/sj/tjgb/202304/P020230412557301980490.pdf. Accessed January 15, 2024.

National Bureau of Statistics of China. National Data. Https://data.stats.gov.cn/english/easyquery.htm. Accessed January 15, 2024.

National Development and Reform Commission of China. *Urgent Notice on Strengthening the Management of the Construction of Maize Processing Projects (Guanyu jiaqiang yumi jiagong xiangmu jianshe guanli de jinji tongzhi).* Beijing: National Development and Reform Commission, 2006.

National Food and Strategic Reserves Administration. "*Notice on Issues Related to the Procurement of National Maize Temporary Storage in Northeast China in 2015 (Guanyu 2015 nian dongbei diqu guojia linshi cunchu yumi shougou youguan wenti de tongzhi).*" Published in September 18, 2015. Http://www.lswz.gov.cn/html/zcfb/2018-06/12/content_216632.shtml. Accessed January 15, 2024.

Office of Technology Evaluation, Department of Commerce, Bureau of Industry and Security of the United States. "2022. U.S. Trade with China." Published 2022. Https://www.bis.doc.gov/index.php/country-papers/3268-2022-statistical-analysis-of-u-s-trade-with-china/file. Accessed January 15, 2024.

Office of the United States Trade Representative. 2018. "*Statement by U.S. Trade Representative Robert Lighthizer on Section 301 Action.*" Https://ustr.gov/about-us/policy-offices/press-office/press-releases/2018/july/statement-us-trade-representative. Accessed January 15, 2024.

World Bank. World Development Indicators. Washington: World Bank. Https://datacatalog.worldbank.org/dataset/world-development-indicators. Accessed January 15, 2024a.

World Bank. *World Integrated Trade Solution.* Https://wits.worldbank.org. Accessed January 15, 2024b.

CHAPTER 4

Economic Growth Dependent on "Ghost" Resources

Abstract This chapter delves into the evolving challenges to China's food issues. The first of these challenges concerns the enduring issue of hunger, which predominantly affects rural populations. The second challenge is China's dietary transition, which began in the 2000s, shifting from a semi-vegetarian diet towards one richer in animal proteins. This shift has heightened the demand for fodder grains, potentially increasing the need for imports. As China's labour supply has peaked and the population has begun to decrease, resource scarcity has become a significant constraint on meeting all domestic grain needs. In this context, China's recently cultivated land totals 127.9 million hectares, just exceeding the 1.8-billion-mu "red line" for basic food needs. This constraint underscores the scarcity of agricultural resources and increases the complexity of achieving food security across all economic sectors in China.

Keywords Food trade • Consumption-production gap • Grain ration needs • The "red line" of arable land • Grain-sown area • Yield level • Food grain • Fodder grain • Virtual land import • The Engel's coefficient • Maize • Soybeans • The United States • Brazil

J. Du, *Farmland, Farming and Food in the National Economy of China, 1947–2020*, Palgrave Studies in Economic History,
https://doi.org/10.1007/978-3-031-70027-9_4

Renewed Concerns on Basic Grain Ration Needs

Food security, often considered as the "people's deity," has been a critical factor in ensuring social stability and is, therefore, an integral element of China's state policy. At its most fundamental level, food security pertains the provision of sufficient calories to sustain the health and productivity of China's population. While it may seem as a routine and often overlooked issue, ensuring food sufficiency remains crucial for the legitimacy of the ruling party.

At the heart of China's food issues is the balance between grain demand and supply. Consequently, a key statistic measure often used to evaluate China's food security situation is per capita grain output. During the Mao era, this benchmark was set at approximately 280 kilogrammes of raw grain per person per year.[1] If we consider roughly 300 kilogrammes per person per year as a proxy for grain self-sufficiency—a level that keeps the Chinese population healthy and productive—China's grain output did not consistently reach this basic level of food security until the 1970s (see Table 4.1).

Indeed, per person food consumption in Mao's China, particularly in the rural sector, was actually lower than the levels observed before the Sino-Japanese War. From the mid-1950s until the late 1970s, the primary driver of increases in China's total food grain supply was the growing population. Until the onset of the opening-up reforms in the 1980s, 80–90% of the daily energy intake for the average Chinese citizen (approximately 2400–2500 kilocalories) still came from the direct consumption of food grains.[2]

[1] Mao claimed that a per capita grain output of 275 kilogrammes was the basic food security line for China. In 1955, Chen Yun confirmed this criterion, stating that 280 kilogrammes of raw grain per head of the rural population was sufficient for all uses, including food consumption, seed and fodder grains.

[2] According to Taylor and Hardde, the average individual energy intake in China was around 2400–2500 kilocalories per day, with approximately 84% of this coming from the direct consumption of food grain. This figure closely matches the dietary structure in China from 1978 to 1989, during which the daily energy intake per person in rural areas consistently remained around 2400–2500 kilocalories. For detailed statistical data, please refer to Ge, Keyou, Chunming Cheng, and Tiefu Sheng. "Food Consumption and Nutritional Status in China." Https://www.fao.org/4/U5900t/u5900t0a.htm. Accessed July 5, 2024; and Taylor, Jeffrey R., and Karen A. Hardee. *Consumer Demand in China: A Statistical Factbook*. Boulder CO: Westview Press, 1986.

Table 4.1 Food requirement of 400 kilogrammes per person per year

		Grain output (Million tonnes)	*Population (Million persons)*	*Per person grain output (Kg/Person)*
		(1)	*(2)*	*(3)*
Mao's Era	1949	113.2	541.7	209.0
	1950	132.1	552.0	239.4
	1951	143.7	563.0	255.2
	1952	163.9	574.8	285.2
	1953	166.8	588.0	283.8
	1954	169.5	602.7	281.3
	1955	183.9	614.7	299.3
	1956	192.8	628.3	306.8
	1957	195.0	646.5	301.7
	1958	197.7	659.9	299.5
	1959	169.7	672.1	252.5
	1960	143.9	662.1	217.3
	1961	136.5	658.6	207.3
	1962	154.4	673.0	229.5
	1963	165.7	691.7	239.6
	1964	180.9	705.0	256.6
	1965	194.5	725.4	268.2
	1966	214.0	745.4	287.1
	1967	217.8	763.7	285.2
	1968	209.1	785.3	266.2
	1969	211.0	806.7	261.5
	1970	240.0	829.9	289.1
	1971	250.1	852.3	293.5
	1972	240.5	871.8	275.9
		Mao's 280 kilogrammes per person per year food security line		
	1973	264.9	892.1	297.0
	1974	275.3	908.6	303.0
	1975	284.5	924.2	307.9
	1976	286.3	937.2	305.5
	1977	282.7	949.7	297.7
	1978	304.8	962.6	316.6

(*continued*)

Table 4.1 (continued)

		Grain output (Million tonnes)	*Population (Million persons)*	*Per person grain output (Kg/Person)*
		(1)	*(2)*	*(3)*
The Dengist Reforms	1979	332.1	975.4	340.5
	1980	320.6	987.1	324.8
	1985	379.1	1058.5	358.2
	1990	446.2	1143.3	390.3
	1995	466.6	1211.2	385.2
	2000	462.2	1267.4	364.7
	2005	484.0	1307.6	370.2
	2006	498.0	1314.5	378.9
	2007	504.1	1321.3	381.6
		400 Kilogrammes per person per year food security line		
	2008	534.3	1328.0	402.4
	2009	539.4	1334.5	404.2
	2010	559.1	1340.9	417.0
	2011	588.5	1349.2	436.2
	2012	612.2	1359.2	450.4
	2013	630.5	1367.3	461.1
	2014	639.6	1376.5	464.7
	2015	660.6	1383.3	477.6
	2016	660.4	1392.3	474.3
	2017	661.6	1400.1	472.5
	2018	657.9	1405.4	468.1
	2019	663.8	1410.1	470.8
	2020	669.5	1412.1	474.1
	2021	682.8	1412.6	483.4
	2022	686.5	1411.8	486.3

Source: National Bureau of Statistics of China. ***China Statistical Yearbook (Zhongguo tongji nianjian).*** Beijing: China Statistics Press (Zhongguo tongji chuban she), 1981–2023 editions; National Bureau of Statistics of China. National Data. Https://data.stats.gov.cn/english/easyquery.htm. Accessed January 15, 2024

If we further consider the energy intake conversion from wheat and rice, which ranges from 2800 to 3340 kilocalories per kilogramme of raw grain,[3] a daily intake of 2500 kilocalories equates to an annual demand of

[3] The conversion rates provided by the Food and Agriculture Organisation were used to calculate ration grain needs. For details, please refer to the Food and Agriculture Organisation. "Food Composition in Terms of the Retail Weight ("As Purchased") in 100 Grams for International Use." Https://www.fao.org/4/X9892E/X9892e05.htm. Accessed July 5, 2024.

273–325 kilogrammes of raw grain per person. This conversion closely aligns with Mao's minimum food security criterion of 280 kilogrammes of raw grain per person per year during the 1950s to 1970s. Consequently, the Chinese population was maintained at merely a subsistence level.

From the 1980s to the mid-2000s, the Chinese government primarily focused on boosting food output to meet China's basic food supply needs and achieve self-sufficiency in staple grain production. As a result, the primary policy objectives emphasised in the government's phased plans and frameworks were to increase food output. It was not until 2009 that China experienced a significant shift in consumption patterns, as the Engel's coefficient for its rural citizens fell below 40%[4] for the first time, classifying the country among developing countries with a better standard of living. This decline, coupled with substantial GDP growth and improved living standards, has transformed the aspirations of the Chinese population. Today, the average daily nutritional intake in China has increased to 4871 kilocalories per person,[5] while the proportion of direct grain consumption has significantly decreased. As a result, the dietary habits of the Chinese people have shifted towards a more varied, protein-based diet, with a higher demand for meat, fish and dairy products.

However, this shift has not eased the pressure on grain farmers. On the contrary, it has increased China's overall food requirements due to the rising demand for grain used as fodder. Typically, it takes between four to seven kilogrammes of raw grain to produce one kilogramme of red meat,[6] necessitating greater grain production to meet this growing demand. Under these new conditions, the benchmark criterion for basic food security has risen from 280 kilogrammes to 400 kilogrammes per person per year (see Table 4.1). These changes have catalysed a shift in policy focus

[4] In 2009, the Engel's coefficient for rural Chinese was 38.0%, slightly lower than the 38.6% recorded for urban Chinese attained in 2000.

[5] Ministry of Agriculture of China. *China Food and Nutrition Development Report 2023*. Beijing: Ministry of Agriculture of China, 2023.

[6] The conversion rates from fodder grain to meat and meat products vary depending on the method used. As mentioned in Chap. 2, the United States Grain Council applies a rate of 6–12 kilogrammes of fodder grain to produce 1 kilogramme of red meat. In contrast, a lower and commonly cited conversion rate provided by *Global Agriculture* is between 4–7 kilogrammes of raw grain to produce 1 kilogramme of red meat. For more details, see Global Agriculture. "Agriculture at a Crossroads: Findings and Recommendations for Future Farming. Https://www.globalagriculture.org/report-topics/meat-and-animal-feed.html." Accessed July 5, 2024.

away from merely increasing food production.[7] Since the mid-2000s, there has been a fundamental change in China's approach to food policy; the focus partly shifted from increasing food production to emphasising farmland protection,[8] aiming to preserve basic agricultural productivity amid industrialisation (Table 4.2).

While improved yield levels have enhanced China's ability to sustain its basic ration needs, new food security issues have begun to emerge. The Fifth Plenum Session of the 19th Central Committee of the CCP introduced a set of reform programmes to address these challenges.[9] The shift in focus from institutional arrangements to productivity preservation in agriculture (see Table 4.2) highlights the fact that food security in China today involves a far more intricate set of challenges.

- The first major challenge is addressing poverty,[10] which still affected well over 55.1 million people[11] in China as of 2019.[12] Despite the

[7] In every Five-Year Plan, food output and supply have consistently been prioritised within the central policy-making framework. However, two distinct structural changes occurred in the 2000s and 2010s due to China's rapidly increasing per capita income and the resulting dietary transition (see Table 4.2).

[8] In addition, during the 12th Five-Year Plan (2011–2015), Beijing introduced a food safety standard to support the development of regulatory systems. This initiative was reinforced by a commitment to enhance the country's legislative framework for food safety, with new rules aimed at addressing food safety issues. In the subsequent 13th Five-Year Plan (2016–2020), a new system for food safety regulation was implemented, establishing a unified framework for national food safety standards and a science-based regulatory mechanism.

[9] For detailed information, refer to the Fifth Plenary Session of the Nineteenth Central Committee of the CCP. *Circular on the Suggestions of the Committee Document on Making the 14th Five-Year Plan for National Economic and Social Development and a Long-Term Objective for 2035 (Zhonggong zhongyang guanyu zhiiding guomin jingji he shehui fazhan di shisi ge wu nian guihua he 2035 nian yuanjing mubiao di jianyi)*. Beijing: Central Committee of the CCP, October 29, 2020.

[10] State Council of China's "Gazette No. 16 of 2020. *Premier Li Keqiang Attended the Press Conference and Answered Questions from Domestic and Foreign Reporters (Likeqiang zongli chuxi jizhe hui bing huida zhongwai jizhe tiwen)*." Beijing: State Council of China, May 28, 2020. Https://www.gov.cn/gongbao/content/2020/content_5517496.htm. Accessed August 15, 2023.

[11] National Bureau of Statistics of China. *Statistical Bulletin of the National Economic and Social Development of the People's Republic of China 2019 (Zhonghua renmin gongheguo 2019 nian guomin jingji he shehui fazhan tongji gongbao)*. Published February 28, 2020. Https://www.gov.cn/xinwen/2020-02/28/content_5484361.htm. Accessed January 15, 2024.

[12] Food and Agriculture Organisation. *The State of Food Security and Nutrition in the World 2020: Transforming Food Systems for Affordable Healthy Diets*. Published in 2020. Https://www.fao.org/3/ca9692en/ca9692en.pdf. Accessed January 15, 2024.

Table 4.2 Food-related issues in China's Five-Year Plans

Five-Year Plans	*Keywords*	*Major targets*	*Achievements*
(1)	(2)	(3)	(4)
1st (1953–1957)[a]	Grain output and supply.	Agricultural GDP to increase by 23.3% in total.	Grain output increased by 17.6%; cotton output increased by 25.4%.
2nd (1958–1962)		Agricultural GDP to increase by 35.0% in total.	Agricultural GDP decreased by 19.9%.
3rd (1966–1970)		Grain output to attain 215–230 million tonnes.	Grain output reached 240.0 million tonnes.
4th (1971–1975)		Grain output to attain 300–325 million tonnes.	Grain output reached 284.5 million tonnes.
5th (1976–1980)		Grain output to attain 325 million tonnes.	Grain output reached 320.6 million tonnes.
6th (1981–1985)		Agricultural GDP to attain 266 billion yuan.	Agricultural GDP reached 254.2 billion yuan.
7th (1986–1990)		Agricultural GDP to increase at an average yearly rate of 4.0%.	Agricultural GDP increased at an average yearly rate of 16.3%.
8th (1991–1995)		Agricultural GDP to attain 878 billion yuan.	Agricultural GDP reached 120.2 billion yuan.
9th (1996–2000)		Grain output to attain 462.5 million tonnes.	Grain output reached 462.2 million tonnes.
10th (2001–2005)		Ensure total area of arable land above 128 million hectares; agricultural GDP to attain 1600 billion yuan.	Total area of arable land was 122.1 million hectares by 2005; agricultural GDP reached 218.1 billion yuan.
11th (2006–2010)	Food safety system; "Redline" of arable land.	Ensure total area of arable land above 120 million hectares; start the implementation of industry nurturing agriculture policy; set up food safety monitoring system.	Total area of arable land in China was 135.3 million hectares by 2010; started to distribute producer subsidies to the farmers; Earmarked 5.5 billion yuan in food safety.
12th (2011–2015)		Sustain food self-sufficiency; built up of food safety monitoring system; Red line of 1.8 billion Chinese mu of arable land.	Per capita food output reached 444 kilogrammes in 2014; total area of arable land was 135.4 million hectares in 2013; initial set-up of a national unified system for food safety monitoring.

(continued)

Table 4.2 (continued)

Five-Year Plans	*Keywords*	*Major targets*	*Achievements*
13th (2016–2020)	"Redline" of arable land; agricultural productivity; rural property rights.	Adhere to the "red line" of arable land; further develop food safety monitoring system; farmland property rights reform.	Per capita food output increased to 474.1 kilogrammes in 2020; total area of arable land was 127.9 million hectares by the end of 2019.
14th (2021–2025)		Adhere to the "red line" of arable land; agricultural technology promotion; rural land property rights reform; speed up urbanisation.	

Source: Ministry of Natural Resources, National Bureau of Statistics and Office of the Second National Land Survey Leading Group of the State Council. ***Bulletin on the Main data of the Second National Land Survey (Guanyu di er ci quanguo tudi diaocha zhuyao shuju chengguo de gongbao)***. Https://www.mnr.gov.cn/zt/hd/dqr/48dqr/zygq/201312/t20131230_2060666.html. Accessed January 15, 2024; National Bureau of Statistics of China. National Data. Https://data.stats.gov.cn/english/easyquery.htm. Accessed January 15, 2024; National Bureau of Statistics of China. ***China Statistical Yearbook (Zhongguo tongji nianjian)***. Beijing: China Statistics Press (Zhongguo tongji chuban she), 1981–2023 editions; Office of the Third National Land Survey Leading Group of the State Council, Ministry of Natural Resources and National Bureau of Statistics of China. ***Bulletin on the Main data of the Third National Land Survey (Di san ci quanguo guotu diaocha zhuyao shuju gongbao)***. Published August 26, 2021. Https://www.gov.cn/xinwen/2021-08/26/content_5633490.htm. Accessed January 15, 2024

Notes: [a]After its establishment, China embarked on a socialist transformation in the early 1950s. The First Five-Year Plan, supported by the former Soviet Union, prioritised industrial growth, with a particular emphasis on heavy industry. Although the First Five-Year Plan successfully increased China's grain output and restored agricultural production to pre-war levels, these achievements were largely due to efficiency improvements from the reorganisation of rural production forms and increased labour input through collective farming. For a detailed discussion of the reforms related to rural production forms, see Chap. 1

annual per person grain output reaching 474.1 kilogrammes in 2020, about four per thousand of the population[13] were still experiencing insufficient food intake. As emphasised by Xi Jinping's statement, "the Chinese people's bowls must be filled with Chinese

[13]In 2019, the Chinese population reached 1410.1 million. Of this total, 55.1 million people, representing 3.9‰ of the population for that year.

grain,"[14] food self-sufficiency has been re-emphasised on the CCP's agenda.[15] This signals that fulfilling the basic grain needs of the entire Chinese population remains a core challenge and a pressing issue.

- Another significant challenge is meeting the changing dietary aspirations of an increasingly urbanising population.[16] The transition from semi-vegetarian diets to those heavily reliant on animal products raises the demand for fodder, thereby necessitating greater crop production and supply by farmers. This trend is already evident in China's agriculture. For example, the sown area of maize experienced an annual growth rate of 2.7% from 1979 to 2021, while the acreage dedicated to wheat and rice declined by 0.5% and 0.3%, respectively.[17] To ensure a steady supply of food grains and support the dietary transition of the Chinese population, there is a heightened emphasis

[14] In recent years, Xi Jinping has continuously emphasised the priority of China's food self-sufficiency. This focus can be traced back to a Party Central Committee rural work meeting on December 23rd, 2013. At this meeting, Xi declared, "Chinese people's bowl must be firmly held in our own hands, and mainly filled with Chinese grains. Only when a country achieves food self-sufficiency can it proactively ensure food security." For more details on Xi's remarks, refer to the report by Xinhua News Agency. "Xi Jinping and Li Keqiang delivered important speeches at central rural work conference (Zhongyang nongcun gongzuo huiiyi juxing xijiinping, likeqiang zuo zhongyao jianghua)." Published December 24, 2013. Https://www.gov.cn/ldhd/2013-12/24/content_2553842.htm. Accessed January 15, 2024.

[15] The Chinese government is likely to face growing challenges in upholding its long-established objective of maintaining a 95% self-sufficiency rate for food ration needs. This goal includes ensuring a self-sufficiency rate of above 95% for rice, wheat and maize, with an ambition to achieve 100% grain self-sufficiency for wheat and rice—China's two most important staple grains. For more insights, refer to Routers. *Chinese Agriculture: Adhere to the Red Line of 95% Food Self-Sufficiency Rate, and not Engage in "De-Ruralisation" in the New Rural Construction—Minister of Agriculture (Zhongguo nongye: Jianchi 95% liangshi ziji lv hongxian, xin nongcun jianshe bu gao "qu nongcun hua"—nongye buzhang)*. Published December 25, 2013. Https://jp.reuters.com/article/idCNL3S0K40ZP20131225. Accessed January 15, 2024.

[16] The dietary transition among the Chinese population began in the 2000s. When per capita income surpassed the upper-middle-income threshold in 2009, this transition accelerated. This increased the demand for fodder grains, such as maize and soybean meal, within China's domestic animal husbandry sector reflected this shift in dietary preferences.

[17] In 2021, the sown area for maize in China expanded to 43.3 million hectares, up from 20.1 million hectares in 1979. Conversely, during the same period, the sown area for rice decreased from 33.9 million hectares to 29.9 million hectares. Similarly, the sown area for wheat also saw a reduction, falling from 29.4 million hectares to 23.7 million hectares. For more detailed data, refer to the National Bureau of Statistics of China. National Data. Https://data.stats.gov.cn/english/easyquery.htm. Accessed January 15, 2024.

on maintaining the "red line" for arable land[18] designated for major staple food crops, a policy that is strictly enforced.

These renewed emphases on food-related issues outlined in the 14th Five-Year Plan[19] (Table 4.2) indicate Beijing's concerns about the obstacles it may face in achieving its overall food security goals. Clearly, China's grain sector has not only reaffirmed its critical importance but also integrated these elements into its politico-economic strategy.

Farmland Constraints and Rural Labour Outflows

The current food security requirement—the minimum food demand per person per year—has been raised to approximately 400 kilogrammes of grain (Table 4.1).[20] Given the size of the Chinese population, this necessitates that, to meet the goal of ensuring that "our bowls should be filled

[18] The core objective of the "Outline of National Land Use Master Plan (2006–2020)" was to safeguard China's 1.8 billion mu (approximately 120 million hectares) of arable land. The master plan stipulated that by 2020, the total area of arable land reserves must not fall below 1.8 billion mu to maintain that the basic farmland needs do not dip below 1.6 billion mu. Following the implementation of the "Master Plan," the goal of ensuring 1.8 billion mu of total cultivated land became a widely accepted benchmark. In 2008, the government officially designated this figure as a "red line" for China's essential farmland reserves. This strategic policy was aimed to ensure staple food self-sufficiency, particularly for wheat and rice. For further information, refer to the State Council of China. "*Document No. 33 of 2008. Notice of the State Council on Issuing the Outline of National Land Use Master Plan 2006–2020 (Guowuyuan guanyu yinfa quanguo tudi liyong zongti guihua gangyao 2006–2020 nian de tongzhi).*" Beijing: State Council of China, October 6, 2008.

[19] See Chapter 53, Section 1 in the Fourth Session of the 13th National People's Congress of China. *The 14th Five-Year Plan for National Economic and Social Development of the People's Republic of China and the Outline of Long-Term Goals for 2035 (Zhonghua renmin gongheguo guomin jingji he shehui fazhan di shisi ge wu nian guihua he 2035 nian yuanjing mubiao gangyao).* Beijing: National People's Congress of China, March 13, 2021.

[20] The Food and Agriculture Organisation of the United States initially set the food security threshold for grain consumption at 400 kilogrammes per person per year. This benchmark has since been adopted by China and is now used as a criterion for measuring food security within the country. For more details, see *China Daily*. "More Efforts Ensure National Food Security." Published on October 18, 2022. Http://english.www.gov.cn/statecouncil/ministries/202210/18/content_WS634dfc66c6d0a757729e1631.html. Accessed January 15, 2024.

mainly with Chinese grain,"[21] China must produce a minimum of 560 million tonnes of food grain throughout the 2020s.[22]

The strong output record of 686.5 million tonnes of grain in 2022 (Table 4.1, Column 1) demonstrates China's capacity to meet the required grain output for food self-sufficiency, provided that other complementary conditions are satisfied. Nevertheless, caution is advised due to the observed fluctuations in per capita grain output since 1979. These fluctuations challenge the optimistic assumptions that the 400-kilogramme per person annual target has been consistently met since 2008.[23] Per capita grain output approached and attained self-sufficiency levels around 1990, only to subsequently decline (Table 4.1, Column 3).

From a long-term perspective, the shift from a semi-vegetarian to a predominantly animal-product-based diet has intensified the demand for fodder grains, compelling farmers to produce more grain crops. Thus, accommodating the ever-increasing need for both food and fodder grains, while ensuring the cultivation of essential staple grain crops, has become more pressing.

An analysis of cereal production since 1979 reveals robust growth in output for all three major cereals: rice, wheat and maize.[24] Maize leads the

[21] Also see Footnote 187. For Xi Jinping's views on China's food security issues, refer to the publication by the Party Literature Research Centre of the Communist Party of China. *Excerpts from Xi Jinping's Exposition on National Food Security.* Beijing: Central Party Literature Press, 2023; and Xinhua News Agency. "Xi Jinping and Li Keqiang Delivered Important Speeches at Central Rural Work Conference (Zhongyang nongcun gongzuo huiyi juxing xijiinping, likeqiang zuo zhongyao jianghua)." Published December 24, 2013. Https://www.gov.cn/ldhd/2013-12/24/content_2553842.htm. Accessed January 15, 2024.

[22] According to the World Bank's population projections, the Chinese population was projected to reach and stabilise at around 1.4 billion in the 2020s. To keep pace with this demographic projection and achieve the targets set forth in the Beijing's food security plan, China's agricultural sector is tasked with producing approximately 559.6 million tonnes of food grain. For additional information on global population projections, refer to the World Bank's data estimates for 2023. World Bank. Population Estimates and Projections. Last modified December 22, 2023. Https://datacatalog.worldbank.org/dataset/population-estimates-and-projections. Accessed January 15, 2024.

[23] The per capita grain output surpassed the food security line, reaching 408 kilogrammes in 2010.

[24] The four major grain crops in China are rice, wheat, maize and soybean. As most soybean consumption in China relies on imports, the acreage allocated to domestic soybean production is relatively small compared to rice, wheat and maize. In 2022, the sown area for soybeans accounted for only 6.0% of total sown area in China, compared to 58.4% for rice, 13.8% for wheat and 25.3% for maize. Therefore, the discussion on land constraints for grain production focuses primarily to rice, wheat and maize.

pack with a maximum annual growth rate of 8.4%, followed by wheat at 2.8% and rice at 1.1%.[25] This trend is encouraging, particularly since maize, the fastest-growing cereal, serves as the primary source of animal fodder in China. Production of rice and wheat peaked in 1998 and was only re-attained in the 2010s. Rather than substantial increases in yields, maize's impressive performance is primarily attributed to the expansion of its sown area, which is partly due to land being reallocating from rice and wheat cultivation.

This shift has palpably reflected in the recent dynamics of China's agriculture, where a notable expansion in the maize production area accelerated in the 2000s (see Fig. 4.1, Panel a). From 1979 to 2021, land allocation to maize production witnessed a yearly growth rate of 2.7%, while the acreage dedicated to wheat and rice declined by 0.5% and 0.3%, respectively.[26]

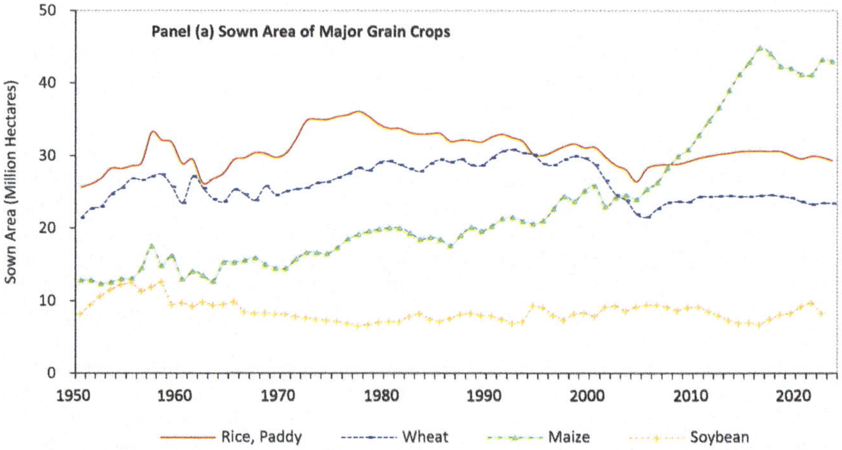

Fig. 4.1 Sown area of major grain crops

[25] From 1979 to 2021, China's maize output rose from 60.0 million tonnes to 272.6 million tonnes. During the same period, wheat production increased from 62.7 million tonnes to 136.9 million tonnes, while rice production rose from 143.8 million tonnes to 212.8 million tonnes.

[26] Here, "growth rates" refer to the average year-on-year change rate calculated over the period from 1979 to 2021.

Should the production of maize, wheat and rice continues to increase, the scarcity of available land in China will heighten the imperative for yield-enhancing technologies. Without the advent of groundbreaking agricultural innovations as significant as the Green Revolution in the future, China will face growing challenges in reallocating farmland to boost maize production.

Thus, it is premature to conclude that China has reached a stable state of food security. Despite the ongoing cycle of food production, China's food self-sufficiency is hindered by several serious challenges. For example, the availability of arable land[27] has experienced a decline (Fig. 4.2). Therefore, assuming that China has already achieved sustainable food security would be overly optimistic.

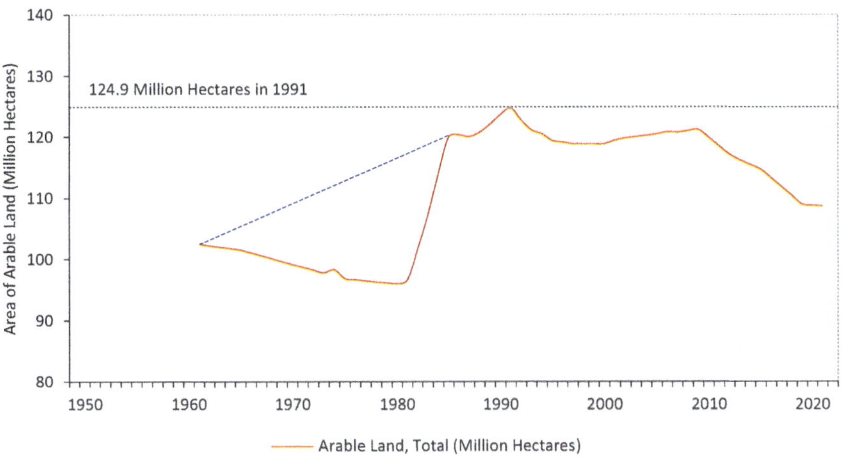

Fig. 4.2 Total area of arable land in China

[27] In the late Qing Dynasty, estimates suggest that Qing China had a minimum of 100 million hectares of arable land (Shi, 2017). Some research even indicates this figure could have reached 130 million hectares by the late eighteenth century (Zheng, Ma, and Wang, 1998). For further details, see Shi, Zhihong. *Agricultural Development in Qing China: A Quantitative Study, 1661–1911*. Leiden: Brill Academic Publishers, 2017; and Zheng, Zheng, Li Ma, Xingping Wang. "China's Real Cropland Area in Qing Dynasty (Qingchao de zhenshi gengdi mianji)." *Jianghai Academic Journal (Jianghai xuekan)* 4 (1998): 129–135.

In 2021, the size of arable land in China was reported to have decreased to 108.9 million hectares,[28] according to the World Bank's World Development Indicators. This figure falls 11.1 million hectares short of the well-known red line of 1.8 billion mu of arable land. However, China's latest official data on cultivated land presents a higher figure of 127.9 million hectares,[29] exceeding the World Bank's estimate. Critics have argued that discrepancies between these data sources may have led to an underestimation of China's total arable land area. These concerns have been addressed through recent advancements in remote sensing and drone technologies, which have provided more accurate measurements. Despite variations in reported figures, it is clear that China's total area of arable land, as a percentage of its total land area, has contracted by around 1.7% since the early 1990s.[30]

The rapid processes of industrial growth and urbanisation have led to a substantial reduction in farmland due to the growing needs for non-agricultural land uses. However, the impact on potential grain output loss is even more critical than the mere loss of farmland.

Alongside rapid urbanisation and growing industrial wages, rural labour outflows have accelerated. In 2019, before the COVID-19 lockdowns in China, rural per capita income shared only about 37.7% of urban income. This significant income gap was primarily driven by the low returns to agricultural production, particularly grain cultivation. As of today, approximately two-thirds of the total sown area in China is devoted to grain cultivation, and about three-quarters of rural labour inputs are involved in grain-related works. This suggests that grain cultivation still constitutes the majority share of rural Chinese productive income (*shengchan xing shouru*).

[28] World Bank. Population Estimates and Projections. Last modified December 22, 2023. Https://datacatalog.worldbank.org/dataset/population-estimates-and-projections. Accessed January 15, 2024.

[29] Office of the Third National Land Survey Leading Group of the State Council, Ministry of Natural Resources, and National Bureau of Statistics of China. *Bulletin on the Main data of the Third National Land Survey (Di san ci quanguo guotu diaocha zhuyao shuju gongbao)*. Published August 26, 2021. Https://www.gov.cn/xinwen/2021-08/26/content_5633490.htm. Accessed January 15, 2024.

[30] In 1991, cultivated land constituted 13.3% of China's total land area, but by 2021, this figure decreased to 11.6%. For more detailed data, please refer to the World Bank. Population Estimates and Projections. Last modified December 22, 2023. Https://datacatalog.worldbank.org/dataset/population-estimates-and-projections. Accessed January 15, 2024.

Since the opening-up reforms, real rural per capita income from grain cultivation has increased by approximately five times, which contrasts sharply with the 30-fold increase in China's real GDP. Alongside government-led urbanisation and shrinking farmland, grain cultivation faces serious constraints due to insufficient land and labour inputs.

This trend is particularly evident in highly productive regions such as Eastern Coastal China. As depicted in Fig. 4.3, the area sown with grain crops in Eastern Costal China has exhibited a consistent downward trend since the 1970s, despite maintaining competitive per-hectare grain yields. A similar trend is also observed in the Western and Central areas of China. The high levels of industrial growth in these areas result in rural per capita income consistently being lower than that in the urban sector. Despite significant labour outflows to the urban sector in search of higher wages, many people remaining in rural areas have turned to local non-agricultural activities, such as online business, to increase their income. This shift has significantly reduced effective labour input and effort in grain production.

While China has a strong track record in agricultural research and development, leading to technical progress and increased grain yields per hectare,[31] these advancements have only partially mitigated the negative impacts of limited farmland and rural labour outflows. The degradation of land quality, coupled with the reductions in both acreage and rural labour, presents formidable obstacles to China's agricultural sustainability.

Should there be no significant advancements in agricultural technology in the near future, the effectiveness of current policies aimed at encouraging higher birth rates could exacerbate the impact of land and agricultural labour constraints on food needs. Against this backdrop, ensuring an adequate grain supply remains a central concern in Beijing's long-term food objectives.

[31] For detailed information, refer to Chapters 23 and 24 in the 14th Five-Year Plan. Fourth Session of the 13th National People's Congress of China. *The 14th Five-Year Plan for National Economic and Social Development of the People's Republic of China and the Outline of Long-Term Goals for 2035 (Zhonghua renmin gongheguo guomin jingji he shehui fazhan di shisi ge wu nian guihua he 2035 nian yuanjing mubiao gangyao)*. Beijing: National People's Congress of China, March 13, 2021.

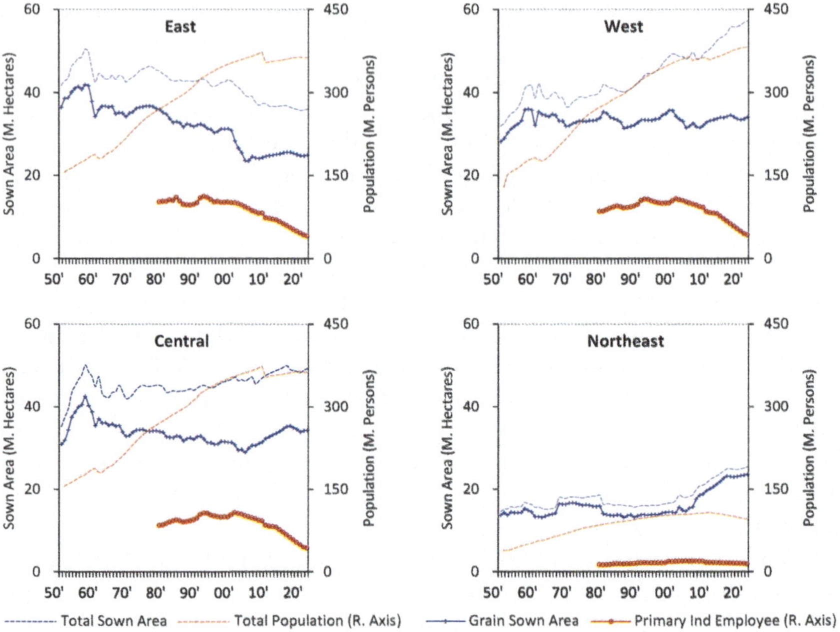

Fig. 4.3 Changes in sown area and primary industry employees in sub-regional China

So far, the East Asian household-based planning model remains heavily reliant on land and labour inputs. With the limited availability of arable land and ongoing urbanisation, Beijing may find it increasingly difficult to bridge the production-consumption gap for fodder grain. In striving to uphold its long-standing policy of achieving self-sufficiency in staple foods, China may need to turn to the international commodity market to address shortfalls in fodder supply. This necessity will require a shift towards greater dependence on global trade to meet national food needs. Consequently, China's expanding involvement in the global grain commodity market has raised concerns about its growing reliance on external trade to sustain the national economy.

Economic Growth Dependent on "Ghost Resources"

China has generally achieved a strong level of self-sufficiency in its staple food supply, with rice and wheat production growing steadily faster than the population increase. In addition to rice and wheat, maize production has seen exceptional growth, driven by rising demand for animal fodder due to dietary changes. Recent per capita cereal availability in China has remained higher than, or close to, global averages for wheat. The potential for further increases in major grain crop output depends on sustaining higher grain yields, which can be achieved through the adoption of agricultural technologies. However, unlike its domestic production capabilities for rice and wheat, China relies on imported maize and soybeans to meet its consumption needs. This reliance, particularly on soybean imports, represents a departure from the domestic self-sufficiency achieved with other crops.

China's domestic per capita grain output has notably shifted its focus from food grains to fodder grains. Predictably, a substantial portion of recent food concerns has been directed towards the cultivation of fodder grain crops. This implies that if China aims to achieve self-sufficiency in fodder grain production, it will need to significantly expand its cultivation area.

In 2021, the sown area for China's four major crops—rice, wheat, maize and soybeans—totalled 105.2 million hectares. Current agricultural technologies and practices, such as monocropping for soybeans, raise questions about China's cultivation pattern, particularly if there is an intention to substitute all maize and soybean imports with domestic production. Assuming China's total arable land remains at 127.6 million hectares amidst ongoing urbanisation in the near future, reducing dependence on fodder grain imports would necessitate reallocating input resources from rice and wheat.

Unlike trade in manufactured products, food imports more directly reflect domestic scarcity in per capita resource endowments. When China can significantly influence the global industrial product market, its growing dependence on "ghost resources" has raised acute concerns about potential risks to the country's ongoing transition.

Ghost Resources Used Through Food Imports

The concept of "ghost" resources was first introduced by Georg Borgström. In his 1962 work,[32] Borgström used the term "ghost acreage" to describe the extent of overseas land required to supplement domestic production with foreign resources through imports. A classical case analysed by Eric Johns[33] was the land that Britain gained in its colonies in the Americas. Although the use of overseas land led to an ecological reliance on foreign capital and natural resources, it significantly helped Britain overcome its resource constraints and support a thriving domestic economy.

In many cases, countries that were once self-sufficient have often surpassed their capacity to produce enough food to sustain autarky, making imports from other countries necessary. With the acceleration of industrialisation and urbanisation, the resource and environmental constraints of China's food production have become increasingly severe, limiting the potential to boost food output through additional resource inputs alone. For a populous country like China, relying solely on domestic resource-led output growth is not sustainable. When domestic production falls short of achieving food autarky, imports become necessary to bridge the gap. Importing food products provides an essential supplement to domestic resources and can indirectly support growth in the country's industrial and service sectors by reallocating saved production resources.

Current research on the factors contributing to growth typically employs productivity analysis to decompose the roles of physical inputs and new technologies within the neo-classical framework. In particular, agricultural production analysis often focuses on: (1) labour and land

[32] The term "ghost acreage" was first introduced by Georg Borgström. It refers to the amount of extra land needed, equivalent to a country's import of foreign foodstuffs, to complement its domestic agricultural production. For further details, see Borgström, Georg. *The Hungry Planet: The Modern World at the Edge of Famine*. New York: Macmillan, (1962) 1965: Ch 5.

[33] Jones, Eric. *The European Miracle: Environments, Economies, and Geopolitics in the History of Europe and Asia*. New York: Cambridge University Press, 1981: Ch 4.

inputs; (2) seed, pesticides and fertilisers[34]; (3) machinery and energy consumption[35]; and (4) technical and institutional changes.[36]

Considering the "technological and institutional changes" as given, the physical inputs equivalent to imports can be derived from China's domestic production forms. In other words, a cost-benefit analysis of China's domestic grain production can reveal how much resource expenditure has been saved by importing major grain crops. To understand the scale of imported grain relative to the domestic input structure, Table 4.3 outlines

[34] Literatures on the input of pesticide and fertilisers on agricultural output include studies by Fan (1997; 2000); Lin (1992); Ma, Calkins, and Johnson (1988); Stone (1993) and Wong (1986). For details, see Fan, Shenggen. "How Fast Have China's Agricultural Production and Productivity Really Been Growing?: New Measurement and Evidence." *International Food Policy Research Institute EPTD Discussion Papers* 30 (1997); Fan, Shenggen. "Technological Change, Technical and Allocative Efficiency in Chinese Agriculture: The Case of Rice Production in Jiangsu." *Journal of International Development* 12/1 (2000): 1–12; Ma, Nathaniel, Peter Calkins and Johnson Stanley. "Technological and Allocative Efficiency vs. Equity in Shuyang County, Jiangsu: General Household Vs. Specialized Households." In John Longworth (eds.), *China's Rural Development Miracle: With International Comparisons.* St Lucia, Queensland: University of Queensland Press, 1989; Stone, Bruce. "Basic Agricultural Technology under Reform." In Y.Y. Kueh and Robert Ash (eds.), *Economics Trends in Chinese Agriculture.* Oxford: Clarendom Press, 1993; Wong, Lung-Fai. *Agricultural Productivity in the Socialist Countries.* Boulder and London: Westview Press, 1986.

[35] Refer to literatures on the use of new farm machinery, irrigation system and energy consumption in agricultural production. For example, Fan, Shenggen. "Effects of Technological Change and Institutional Reform on Production Growth in Chinese Agriculture." *American Journal of Agricultural Economics* 73(1991): 266–275; Yao, Shujie and Zinan Liu. "Determinants of Grain Production and Technological Efficiency in China." *Journal of Agricultural Economics* 49/2 (1998): 171–184.

[36] Studies on technical and institutional changes examine the impact of technical innovations and agricultural institutions, changes in the market environment and urban-rural economic structure, and new cropping techniques such as the widespread adoption of double cropping system in rice-planting regions since the early reform period. For detailed discussions, please refer to Fan, Shenggen, Linxiu Zhang and Xiaobo Zhang. "Reforms, Investment, and Poverty in Rural China." *Economic Development and Cultural Change* 52/2 (2004): 395–421; Feder, Gershon, Lawrence Lau, Justin Lin and Xiaopeng Luo. "Credit's Effect on Productivity in Chinese Agriculture: A Microeconomic Model of Disequilibrium." *The World Bank Policy Research Working Paper Series* 571 (1991); Huang, Jikun and Scott Rozelle. "Technological Change: Rediscovering the Engine of Productivity Growth in China's Rural Economy." *Journal of Development Economics* 49/2 (1996): 337–369; Jin Songqing, Hengyun Ma, Jikun Huang, Ruifa Hu and Scott Rozelle. "Productivity, Efficiency and Technical Change: Measuring the Performance of China's Transforming Agriculture." *Journal of Productivity Analysis* 33 (2010): 191–207; Lin, Justin. "An Economic Theory of Institutional Change: Induced and Imposed Change." *Cato Journal* 9(1989): 1–33.

the major inputs for China's imports of four key grain crops—rice, wheat, maize and soybeans—over the past two decades of dietary transition.

As is shown in Table 4.3, the import-equivalent labour inputs for rice, wheat and maize are relatively small (Columns 2, 5 and 8). In contrast, the land and capital investment saved through wheat and soybean imports are notably higher (Columns 4,6 and 10,12). Among the four major grain crops, soybean imports account for the largest share of all factor inputs, due to both its substantial import volume and the monocropping planting technique.

With the acceleration of industrialisation and urbanisation, domestic production of the four major grain crops could increasingly be constrained by the availability of farmland. For instance, in 2022, the use of "ghost land"—representing the land equivalent required to produce the net import of these four major grain crops—reached 51.8 million hectares[37] (see Table 4.3). This accounted for 43.5% of China's grain-sown area (119.0 million hectares) and 30.2% of the total sown area (171.6 million hectares) for that year. China's rising per capita income has further exacerbated the domestic supply-consumption gap. Consequently, net imports of major grain crops are expected to continue increasing.

Contribution of Ghost Resources to Non-agricultural Growth

To further understand the role of grain imports in China's industrialisation, a counterfactual estimation is employed to assess how resources saved by grain imports have contributed to China's industrial and service sectors. Given the strict restrictions on the cross-sectoral flow of farmland in China, the focus is on evaluating the contributions of labour and capital to China's growth and development over the past two decades of dietary transition.

Theoretically, in addition to capital (K_{it}) and labour (L_{it}), the portion of output growth not explained by these factor inputs is known as the "Solow residual."[38] The elasticity of each factor input to output growth is crucial for estimating the Solow residual, which revels the contribution of

[37] Compared to the ghost acreage (virtual land) for all food imports discussed in Chap. 3, this section focusses specifically on the four major grain crops in China's food security plan: namely rice, wheat, maize and soybeans.

[38] Solow, Robert M. 1957. "Technical Change and the Aggregate Production Function." *The Review of Economics and Statistics* 39/3 (1957): 312–320.

Table 4.3 Ghost resources used through the imports of four major crops

	Rice, paddy			*Wheat*			*Maize*			*Soybean*			*Grain, total*		
	Land (M. Ha)	Labour (M. Person)	Invest. (M. 2015 US$)	Land (M. Ha)	Labour (M. Person)	Invest. (M. 2015 US$)	Land (M. Ha)	Labour (M. Person)	Invest. (M. 2015 US$)	Land (M. Ha)	Labour (M. Person)	Invest. (M. 2015 US$)	Land (M. Ha)	Labour (M. Person)	Invest. (M. 2015 US$)
	(1)	(2)	(3)	(4)	(5)	(6)	(7)	(8)	(9)	(10)	(11)	(12)	(19)	(20)	(21)
1980	0.03	–	–	5.73	–	–	0.59	–	–	0.52	–	–	6.87		–
1985	0.04	0.05	22.7	1.83	1.59	876.7	0.03	0.02	10.3	0.00	0.00	0.1	1.90	1.67	909.8
1990	0.01	0.01	8.3	3.92	3.29	2544.1	0.08	0.08	48.0	0.00	0.00	0.2	4.01	3.39	2600.5
1995	0.27	0.31	262.7	3.27	2.49	2420.6	1.05	1.01	728.4	0.18	0.11	66.2	4.78	3.93	3477.9
2000	0.04	0.03	31.4	0.23	0.11	222.3	0.00	0.00	0.4	6.29	2.79	2515.4	6.57	2.94	2769.6
2001	0.04	0.04	35.2	0.18	0.10	134.2	0.01	0.01	4.9	8.58	3.81	3340.8	8.81	3.96	3515.1
2002	0.04	0.03	31.8	0.16	0.09	122.7	0.00	0.00	0.9	5.98	2.58	2517.4	6.18	2.70	2672.8
2003	0.04	0.03	34.6	0.11	0.06	78.6	0.00	0.00	0.2	12.55	5.65	5492.5	12.70	5.74	5605.8
2004	0.12	0.09	99.7	1.70	0.83	1253.1	0.00	0.00	0.3	11.15	3.46	4786.8	12.97	4.38	6139.9
2005	0.08	0.06	70.5	0.82	0.39	628.8	0.00	0.00	0.5	15.60	4.78	6283.5	16.50	5.23	6983.2
2006	0.11	0.07	99.4	0.13	0.05	99.9	0.01	0.01	7.9	17.44	4.87	6517.3	17.69	5.00	6724.4
2007	0.07	0.04	63.8	0.02	0.01	14.0	0.01	0.00	4.3	21.20	5.76	7823.4	21.30	5.82	7905.5
2008	0.04	0.02	44.8	0.01	0.00	5.5	0.01	0.00	6.3	21.99	5.13	9910.0	22.05	5.16	9966.5
2009	0.05	0.03	49.5	0.19	0.07	175.9	0.02	0.01	11.3	26.10	6.17	11,108.4	26.36	6.27	11,345.0
2010	0.06	0.03	54.6	0.26	0.09	224.6	0.29	0.13	206.5	30.94	6.37	14,042.2	31.54	6.61	14,528.0
2011	0.09	0.04	89.5	0.26	0.09	234.6	0.30	0.13	239.3	28.57	5.36	13,037.9	29.21	5.62	13,601.4
2012	0.34	0.15	388.4	0.74	0.23	729.2	0.89	0.37	760.0	32.18	5.87	16,377.7	34.15	6.62	18,255.2
2013	0.33	0.14	379.5	1.09	0.33	1104.8	0.54	0.21	475.0	36.01	6.22	17,901.0	37.98	6.90	19,860.3
2014	0.37	0.14	423.4	0.57	0.17	571.6	0.45	0.17	393.0	39.95	6.83	19,524.5	41.34	7.31	20,912.6
2015	0.48	0.18	559.1	0.55	0.15	557.5	0.80	0.29	727.2	45.10	7.25	21,921.2	46.93	7.87	23,764.9
2016	0.51	0.18	590.5	0.62	0.17	645.1	0.53	0.18	465.8	46.90	7.32	22,427.6	48.57	7.84	24,129.0
2017	0.58	0.19	652.7	0.78	0.20	783.1	0.46	0.15	395.2	51.54	7.79	23,684.8	53.36	8.33	25,515.7
2018	0.43	0.14	488.2	0.53	0.13	526.4	0.58	0.17	487.4	46.38	6.40	20,834.3	47.92	6.84	22,336.3
2019	0.35	0.11	404.6	0.57	0.13	581.6	0.76	0.22	643.3	45.69	6.80	18,804.2	47.37	7.26	20,433.7

(continued)

Table 4.3 (continued)

	Rice, paddy			Wheat			Maize			Soybean			Grain, total		
2020	0.41	0.12	483.0	1.42	0.32	1441.8	1.79	0.51	1517.9	50.58	7.19	22,549.0	54.20	8.14	25,991.7
2021	0.69	0.19	814.0	1.67	0.36	1668.6	4.51	1.29	3783.3	49.54	6.78	22,192.2	56.41	8.61	28,458.0
2022	0.87	0.23	1139.3	1.69	0.36	1918.4	3.20	0.87	3105.7	46.00	6.21	23,026.9	51.76	7.67	29,190.4

Source: Department of Price of the National Development and Reform Commission of China. ***National Agricultural Costs and Returns Compilation***. Beijing: China Statistics Press, 2000–2023 editions; Food and Agriculture Organization of the United Nations. FAOSTAT Statistics Database. Https://www.fao.org/faostat/en/#data. Accessed January 15, 2024; World Bank. World Development Indicators. Washington: World Bank. Https://datacatalog.worldbank.org/dataset/world-development-indicators. Accessed January 15, 2024; National Bureau of Statistics of China. National Data. Https://data.stats.gov.cn/english/easyquery.htm. Accessed January 15, 2024

additional labour and capital input to the output growth rate through TFP analysis. While input-output frontier analysis is widely used in productivity studies, it primarily focuses on exploring the Solow Black Box[39] to verify various types of technological changes. For our purpose, this analysis employs a production function-based TFP approach to estimate the contribution of labour and capital inputs saved through imports to China's non-agricultural growth during the dietary transition period.

The Solow residual is thus estimated using the Cobb-Douglas production function[40] as described in Eq. (4.1).

$$Y = Af\left(K,L\right) \tag{4.1}$$

To better observe technical change, the unexplained part of growth is decomposed into $\theta_{it} + e_{it}$, where θ_{it} represents technical change and e_{it} denotes the residual. Assuming that technical change (θ_{it}) is Hicks-neutral,[41] the log-transformed function can be rewritten as shown in Eq. (4.2):

$$y_{it} = \alpha_l l_{it} + \alpha_k k_{it} + \theta_{it} + e_{it} \tag{4.2}$$

Incorporating the Ackerberg-Caves-Frazer method to address endogeneity,[42] the Olley-Pakes model[43] is selected due to its consideration of the complexity of intermediate inputs (m_{it}) in production and the availability of data. Hence, Eq. (4.2) is expanded to include intermediate inputs m_{it}, allowing for the estimation of the expected output $\hat{y}_{it}$ and the unobservable shock component e_{it}, as shown in Eq. (4.3)

[39] For a discussion on Solow Black Box and the decomposition of technical changes, refer to Kumbhakar, Subal C., and Ca Knox Lovell. "Stochastic Frontier Analysis: An Econometric Approach." *European Journal of Operational Research* 80(1995): 452–461; and Nishimizu, Mieko, and John M. Page. "Total Factor Productivity Growth, Technological Progress and Technical Efficiency Changes." *Economic Journal* 92 (1982): 920–936.

[40] See, Cobb, Charles W., and Paul H. Douglas. "A Theory of Production." *The American Economic Review* 18/1 (1928): 139–165.

[41] Hicks, John. *The Theory of Wages*. London: Macmillan, 1932.

[42] Ackerberg, Daniel A., Kevin Caves, and Garth Frazer. "Identification Properties of Recent Production Function Estimators." *Econometrica* 83/6(2015): 2411–2451.

[43] Olley, G. Steven, and Ariel Pakes. 1996. "The Dynamics of Productivity in the Telecommunications Equipment Industry." *Econometrica* 64/6(1996): 1263–1297.

$$y_{it} = \gamma_{it}\left(l_{it}, k_{it}, \theta_{it}, m_{it}\right) + e_{it} \tag{4.3}$$

Accordingly, TFP in China's non-agricultural sectors can be expressed as a function of α_i,

$$\theta_{it}\left(\alpha\right) = \hat{\gamma}_{it} - \alpha_l l_{it} - \alpha_k k_{it} \tag{4.4}$$

Through the estimation of Eq. (4.4), the contribution of each factor input saved from grain imports can be assessed. Firm-level data from non-agricultural companies listed on A-share stock market, collected from the China Stock Market and Accounting Research database,[44] is used for the TFP estimation. Given the acceleration of China's grain imports from the early 2000s due to rapid dietary changes, the observation period is limited to 2000–2022. The data includes: (1) output level, estimated by a firm's operating income; (2) labour input, measured by the number of employees in the observation year; (3) the value of fixed assets as a proxy for capital input in production; and (4) the sum of intermediate inputs, calculated by deducting asset depreciation and wage expenses from the total cost incurred during the observation year. After winsorising the independent variables at the 1st and 99th percentiles, 52,621 observations are retained. Table 4.4 provides a detailed description of the data.

In additional to Olley-Pakes model, Ordinary Least Square and Fixed Effects methods are also applied to estimate Eq. (4.5) for robustness.

$$y_{it} = \alpha_0 + \alpha_l k_{it} + \alpha_k l_{it} + \sum_{i=1}^{n} \beta_1 year_{it} + \sum_{i=1}^{n} \beta_2 area_{it} + \sum_{i=1}^{n} \beta_3 sector_{it} + \varepsilon_{it} \tag{4.5}$$

Table 4.5 presents the results.

All three methods yield relatively close estimates for the contribution of capital and labour in China's non-agricultural productivity. Notably, the contribution of labour exceeds that of capital. From 2000 to 2022, Table 4.5 indicates that labour input contributed between 56.7% and 60.4% to production growth, while capital contributed between 26.2% and 34.1%. This underscores the significant role of labour in China's industrialisation since the 2000s.

[44] China Stock Market and Accounting Research Database. Https://cn.gtadata.com. Accessed January 15, 2024.

Table 4.4 Summary statistics

Var.	*Obs.*	*Mean*	*S.D.*	*Min.*	*Max.*	*Description*
	(1)	*(2)*	*(3)*	*(4)*	*(5)*	*(6)*
y_{it}	52,621	21.26	1.55	15.23	26.13	Log-transformed total operating income.
l_{it}	52,621	7.55	1.32	2.94	11.39	Log-transformed number of employees.
k_{it}	52,621	20.04	1.73	13.53	25.08	Log-transformed net fixed assets.
m_{it}	52,621	21.09	1.54	16.61	25.90	Operating expenses minus asset discount and salaries.
year	52,621	–	–	–	–	The year that observation value belongs to.
sector	52,621	–	–	–	–	The sector that the observation firm belongs to.
area	52,621	–	–	–	–	The province where the observation firm is registered.

Source: Compiled by the author

Table 4.5 Contribution of labour and capital in non-agricultural productivity estimation

	y_{it}		
	Ordinary least square	*Fixed effects*	*Olley–Pakes model*
	(1)	*(2)*	*(3)*
l_{it}	0.567***	0.478***	0.604***
	(0.004)	(0.004)	(0.037)
k_{it}	0.353***	0.262***	0.341***
	(0.003)	(0.003)	(0.007)
Obs.	52,621	52,621	52,621
R^2	0.745	0.704	–

Notes: Standard errors are reported in parentheses; ***p<0.01, **p<0.05, *p<0.1

According to Table 4.3, from 2000 to 2022, the total labour input saved by grain imports amounted to 142.8 million person-years, and the production investment saved totalled 350.6 billion US dollars (in 2015 prices). If China had substituted its grain imports with domestic production during this period, it would have required reallocating 142.8 million person-years of employment and 350.6 billion dollars in social investment away from the industrial and service sectors. These figures represent 1.3%

of total employment and 0.4% of total fixed asset investment in non-agricultural sectors from 2000 to 2022, respectively.

Considering the combined impact of labour and capital saved through imports, their compound contribution to China's non-agricultural GDP growth rate is approximately 17–22% in the last two decades, depending on the TFP method used in estimation. If imports of rapeseeds and cotton are also included in the calculation, this compound contribution rate could reach around a quarter.

Over the past two decades, China has achieved remarkable growth and a high standard of self-sufficiency in meeting its basic food needs.[45] The country had successfully lifted a significant portion of its population out of poverty, and it stands as one of the few globally to have achieved the United Nations' Millennium Development Goals aimed at halving the percentage share of people living with hunger.[46]

However, by the end of 2019, 55.1 million Chinese were still living below the poverty line,[47] affecting more than 3.9 individuals per thousand of the population.[48] Although China has consistently produced more than

[45] Since the initiation of the First Five-Year Plan (1953–1957), which marked the beginnings of China's major industrial development, food security has been regarded as a crucial pillar supporting national industrialisation. Subsequently, food security issues have consistently held a prominent place in central policy-making throughout each Five-Year Plan. From the First Five-Year Plan to the end of the 13th Five-Year Plan (2016–2020), China's grain output grew from 163.9 million tonnes in 1953 to 669.5 million tonnes in 2020. Over the same period, the average annual per person grain output rose from 283.8 kilogrammes to 474.1 kilogrammes, reflecting substantial improvements in agricultural productivity.

[46] The operationalisation of the United Nations' Millennium Development Goals included the establishment of eight time-bound targets to monitor development progress from 1990 to 2015. The primary goal among these was to halve the proportion of the population who were living in hunger by 2015. China's monumental achievement in poverty reduction contributed to nearly two-thirds of the reduction in hunger across developing countries and significantly enhanced East Asia's overall performance in the global fight against hunger. For more detailed information, please refer to the United Nations. *The Millennium Development Goals Report 2015*. Published in 2015. Https://www.un.org/millenniumgoals/2015_MDG_Report/pdf/MDG%202,015%20rev%20(July%201).pdf. Accessed January 15, 2024.

[47] National Bureau of Statistics of China. *Statistical Bulletin of the National Economic and Social Development of the People's Republic of China 2019 (Zhonghua renmin gongheguo 2019 nian guomin jingji he shehui fazhan tongji gongbao)*. Published February 28, 2020. Https://www.gov.cn/xinwen/2020-02/28/content_5484361.htm. Accessed January 15, 2024.

[48] China's poverty line is set at 2300 yuan per person per year (constant 2010 yuan), which is equivalent to 6.3 yuan per day. Even when adjusted for 2011 purchasing power parity, this threshold remains lower than the global poverty line set up by the World Bank at US$1.9 per day. For further details, please refer to the World Bank. Aid Effectiveness Indicators.

400 kilogrammes of grain per person per year, individual grain consumption has increasingly relied on imports. This consumption-production gap has been widening year by year since the 2000s (Fig. 4.4, Panel a). On the one hand, ensuring a basic grain ration for food self-sufficiency remains a persistent challenge for ordinary people; on the other hand, the affluent urban Chinese dietary shift towards higher animal protein consumption has significantly increased the demand for grain for fodder.

The growing consumption-supply gap indicates that China's resources have reached their limits. Particularly as China's labour supply has peaked and the population has begun to decrease,[49] resource scarcity has become a significant constraint on meeting all domestic grain needs if no significant technological advancements occur in the near future.

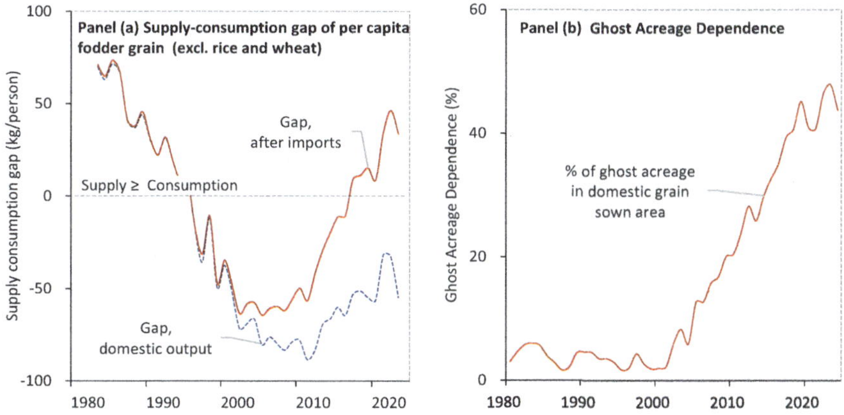

Fig. 4.4 Per capita supply-consumption gap of fodder grain (excl. Rice and wheat) and ghost acreage dependence associated with grain imports

Https://data.worldbank.org/topic/aid-effectiveness. Accessed January 15, 2024; Food and Agriculture Organisation. *The State of Food Security and Nutrition in the World 2020: Transforming Food Systems for Affordable Healthy Diets*. Published in 2020. Https://www.fao.org/3/ca9692en/ca9692en.pdf. Accessed January 15, 2024.

[49] Du, Jane. *China's Labour Market, 1950–2050: The Role of Family Planning in Demographic and Income Transitions*. London: Palgrave Macmillan.

Apart from the labour and capital inputs, farmland is the most essential and irreplaceable resource in food production. As shown in Fig. 4.4, Panel a, the consumption-supply gap for fodder grain has widened. Although the gap narrowed during the 1980s and 1990s, when China's agriculture adopted Green Revolution technologies that rapidly increased domestic yields, it reappeared in the mid-1990s. Since then, the widening consumption-supply gap has continued to worsen until the government resorted to imports. However, the side effect has been a surging dependence of fodder use on ghost acreage (Fig. 4.4, Panel b). Recently, the ghost acreage associated with grain imports has accounted for as much as half of domestic grain-sown area. Any reduction in land availability directly affects grain production capacity. In this context, China's recently cultivated land totals 127.9 million hectares[50] (equivalent to 1.9 billion Chinese mu), just exceeding the 1.8-billion-mu "red line," the minimum threshold required for basic food needs.[51]

Without the support of food imports to alleviate domestic resource constraints over the past two decades, China's recent GDP growth rate could have been 17–22% slower. With food imports, the reliance on imported grain has surged to encompass half of the domestic grain-sown areas or one-third of total sown area in 2022. Alongside the growing demand of fodder grains due to the ongoing dietary transition, the Chinese government almost certainly will find it increasingly challenging to address food security issues domestically, despite its efforts to do so.

References

Ackerberg, Daniel A., Kevin Caves, and Garth Frazer. "Identification Properties of Recent Production Function Estimators." *Econometrica* 83/6 (2015): 2411–2451.

Borgström, Georg. *The Hungry Planet: The Modern World at the Edge of Famine*. New York: Macmillan, 1962 [1965].

[50] Office of the Third National Land Survey Leading Group of the State Council, Ministry of Natural Resources and National Bureau of Statistics of China. *Bulletin on the Main data of the Third National Land Survey (Di san ci quanguo guotu diaocha zhuyao shuju gongbao)*. Published August 26, 2021. Https://www.gov.cn/xinwen/2021-08/26/content_5633490.htm. Accessed January 15, 2024.

[51] However, as mentioned earlier, there is a significant shortfall in arable land area according to World Bank data, with an 11.1-million-hectare deficit compared to the minimum arable land area mandated by the "red line" policy.

China Daily. "More Efforts Ensure National Food Security." Published on 18 October 2022. Http://english.www.gov.cn/statecouncil/ministries/202210/18/content_WS634dfc66c6d0a757729e1631.html. Accessed January 15, 2024.

China Stock Market and Accounting Research Database. Https://cn.gtadata.com. Accessed January 15, 2024.

Department of Comprehensive Statistics of National Bureau of Statistics of China. *China Compendium of Statistics 1949–2008 (Xin Zhongguo 60 nian tongji ziliao huibian)*. Beijing: China Statistics Press (Zhongguo tongji chuban she), 2010.

Department of Price of the National Development and Reform Commission of China. *National Agricultural Costs and Returns Compilation*. Beijing: China Statistics Press, 2000–2023 editions.

Du, Jane. *China's Labour Market, 1950–2050: The Role of Family Planning in Demographic and Income Transitions*. London: Palgrave Macmillan.

Fan, Shenggen, Linxiu Zhang and Xiaobo Zhang. "Reforms, Investment, and Poverty in Rural China." *Economic Development and Cultural Change* 52/2 (2004): 395–421.

Fan, Shenggen. "Effects of Technological Change and Institutional Reform on Production Growth in Chinese Agriculture." *American Journal of Agricultural Economics* 73 (1991): 266–275.

Fan, Shenggen. "How Fast Have China's Agricultural Production and Productivity Really Been Growing?: New Measurement and Evidence." *International Food Policy Research Institute EPTD Discussion Papers* 30 (1997).

Fan, Shenggen. "Technological Change, Technical and Allocative Efficiency in Chinese Agriculture: The Case of Rice Production in Jiangsu." *Journal of International Development* 12/1 (2000): 1–12.

Feder, Gershon, Lawrence Lau, Justin Lin and Xiaopeng Luo. "Credit's Effect on Productivity in Chinese Agriculture: A Microeconomic Model of Disequilibrium." *The World Bank Policy Research Working Paper Series* 571 (1991).

Fifth Plenary Session of the Nineteenth Central Committee of the CCP. *Circular on the Suggestions of the Committee Document on Making the 14th Five-Year Plan for National Economic and Social Development and a Long-Term Objective for 2035 (Zhonggong zhongyang guanyu zhiiding guomin jingji he shehui fazhan di shisi ge wu nian guihua he 2035 nian yuanjing mubiao di jianyi)*. Beijing: Central Committee of the CCP, October 29, 2020.

Food and Agriculture Organisation. "Food Composition in Terms of the Retail Weight ("As Purchased") in 100 Grams for International Use." Https://www.fao.org/4/X9892E/X9892e05.htm. Accessed July 5, 2024a.

Food and Agriculture Organisation. *The State of Food Security and Nutrition in the World 2020: Transforming Food Systems for Affordable Healthy Diets.* Published in 2020. Https://www.fao.org/3/ca9692en/ca9692en.pdf. Accessed January 15, 2024b.

Food and Agriculture Organization of the United Nations. FAOSTAT Statistics Database. Https://www.fao.org/faostat/en/#data. Accessed January 15 2024.

Fourth Session of the 13th National People's Congress of China. *The 14th Five-Year Plan for National Economic and Social Development of the People's Republic of China and the Outline of Long-Term Goals for 2035 (Zhonghua renmin gongheguo guomin jingji he shehui fazhan di shisi ge wu nian guihua he 2035 nian yuanjing mubiao gangyao).* Beijing: National People's Congress of China, March 13, 2021.

Ge, Keyou, Chunming Cheng, and Tiefu Sheng. "Food Consumption and Nutritional Status in China." Https://www.fao.org/4/U5900t/u5900t0a.htm. Accessed July 5, 2024.

Global Agriculture. "Agriculture at a Crossroads: Findings and Recommendations for Future Farming. Https://www.globalagriculture.org/report-topics/meat-and-animal-feed.html. Accessed July 5, 2024.

Hicks, John. *The Theory of Wages.* London: Macmillan, 1932.

Huang, Jikun and Scott Rozelle. "Technological Change: Rediscovering the Engine of Productivity Growth in China's Rural Economy." *Journal of Development Economics* 49/2 (1996): 337–369.

Jin Songqing, Hengyun Ma, Jikun Huang, Ruifa Hu and Scott Rozelle. "Productivity, Efficiency and Technical Change: Measuring the Performance of China's Transforming Agriculture." *Journal of Productivity Analysis* 33 (2010): 191–207.

Jones, Eric. *The European Miracle: Environments, Economies, and Geopolitics in the History of Europe and Asia.* New York: Cambridge University Press, 1981.

Kumbhakar, Subal C., and Ca Knox Lovell. "Stochastic Frontier Analysis: An Econometric Approach." *European Journal of Operational Research* 80 (1995): 452–461.

Lin, Justin Y. "An Economic Theory of Institutional Change: Induced and Imposed Change." *Cato Journal* 9 (1989): 1–33.

Ma, Nathaniel, Peter Calkins and Johnson Stanley. "Technological and Allocative Efficiency vs. Equity in Shuyang County, Jiangsu: General Household Vs. Specialized Households." In John Longworth (eds.), *China's Rural Development Miracle: With International Comparisons.* St Lucia, Queensland: University of Queensland Press, 1989.

Ministry of Agriculture of China. *China Food and Nutrition Development Report 2023.* Beijing: Ministry of Agriculture of China, 2023.

Ministry of Natural Resources, National Bureau of Statistics, and Office of the Second National Land Survey Leading Group of the State Council. *Bulletin on the Main data of the Second National Land Survey (Guanyu di er ci quanguo tudi diaocha zhuyao shuju chengguo de gongbao)*. Https://www.mnr.gov.cn/zt/hd/dqr/48dqr/zygq/201312/t20131230_2060666.html. Accessed January 15, 2024.

National Bureau of Statistics of China. *China Statistical Yearbook (Zhongguo tongji nianjian)*. Beijing: China Statistics Press (Zhongguo tongji chuban she), 1981–2023 editions.

National Bureau of Statistics of China. National Data. Https://data.stats.gov.cn/english/easyquery.htm. Accessed January 15, 2024.

National Bureau of Statistics of China. *Statistical Bulletin of the National Economic and Social Development of the People's Republic of China 2019 (Zhonghua renmin gongheguo 2019 nian guomin jingji he shehui fazhan tongji gongbao)*. Published February 28, 2020. Https://www.gov.cn/xinwen/2020-02/28/content_5484361.htm. Accessed January 15, 2024.

World Bank. Aid Effectiveness Indicators. Https://data.worldbank.org/topic/aid-effectiveness. Accessed January 15, 2024a.

Nishimizu, Mieko, and John M. Page. "Total Factor Productivity Growth, Technological Progress and Technical Efficiency Changes." *Economic Journal* 92 (1982): 920–936.

Office of the Third National Land Survey Leading Group of the State Council, Ministry of Natural Resources, and National Bureau of Statistics of China. *Bulletin on the Main data of the Third National Land Survey (Di san ci quanguo guotu diaocha zhuyao shuju gongbao)*. Published August 26, 2021. Https://www.gov.cn/xinwen/2021-08/26/content_5633490.htm. Accessed January 15, 2024.

Olley, G. Steven, and Ariel Pakes. 1996. "The Dynamics of Productivity in the Telecommunications Equipment Industry." *Econometrica* 64/6 (1996): 1263–1297.

Party Literature Research Centre of the Communist Party of China. *Excerpts from Xi Jinping's Exposition on National Food Security*. Beijing: Central Party Literature Press, 2023.

Routers. *Chinese Agriculture: Adhere to the Red Line of 95% Food Self-Sufficiency Rate, and not Engage in "De-Ruralisation" in the New Rural Construction—Minister of Agriculture (Zhongguo nongye: Jianchi 95% liangshi ziji lv hongxian, xin nongcun jianshe bu gao "qu nongcun hua"—nongye buzhang)*. Published December 25, 2013. Https://jp.reuters.com/article/idCNL3S0K40ZP20131225. Accessed January 15, 2024.

Cobb, Charles W., and Paul H. Douglas. "A Theory of Production." *The American Economic Review* 18/1 (1928): 139–165.

Shi, Zhihong. *Agricultural Development in Qing China: A Quantitative Study, 1661–1911*. Leiden: Brill Academic Publishers, 2017.

Solow, Robert M. 1957. "Technical Change and the Aggregate Production Function." *The Review of Economics and Statistics* 39/3 (1957): 312–320.

State Council of China. "*Document No. 33 of 2008. Notice of the State Council on Issuing the Outline of National Land Use Master Plan 2006–2020 (Guowuyuan guanyu yinfa quanguo tudi liyong zongti guihua gangyao 2006–2020 nian de tongzhi).*" Beijing: State Council of China, October 6, 2008.

State Council of China. "*Gazette No. 16 of 2020. Premier Li Keqiang Attended the Press Conference and Answered Questions from Domestic and Foreign Reporters (Likeqiang zongli chuxi jizhe hui bing huida zhongwai jizhe tiwen).*" Beijing: State Council of China, 28 May 2020. Https://www.gov.cn/gongbao/content/2020/content_5517496.htm. Accessed August 15, 2023.

Stone, Bruce. "Basic Agricultural Technology under Reform." In Y.Y. Kueh and Robert Ash (eds.), *Economics Trends in Chinese Agriculture*. Oxford: Clarendom Press, 1993.

Taylor, Jeffrey R., and Karen A. Hardee. *Consumer Demand in China: A Statistical Factbook*. Boulder CO: Westview Press, 1986.

United Nations. *The Millennium Development Goals Report 2015*. Published in 2015. Https://www.un.org/millenniumgoals/2015_MDG_Report/pdf/MDG%202015%20rev%20(July%201).pdf. Accessed January 15, 2024.

Wong, Lung-Fai. *Agricultural Productivity in the Socialist Countries*. Boulder and London: Westview Press, 1986.

World Bank. Population Estimates and Projections. Last modified December 22, 2023. Https://datacatalog.worldbank.org/dataset/population-estimates-and-projections. Accessed January 15, 2024b.

World Bank. World Development Indicators. Washington: World Bank. Https://datacatalog.worldbank.org/dataset/world-development-indicators. Accessed January 15, 2024c.

Xinhua News Agency. "Xi Jinping and Li Keqiang Delivered Important Speeches at Central Rural Work Conference (Zhongyang nongcun gongzuo huiiyi juxing xijiinping, likeqiang zuo zhongyao jianghua)." Published December 24, 2013. Https://www.gov.cn/ldhd/2013-12/24/content_2553842.htm. Accessed January 15, 2024.

Yao, Shujie and Zinan Liu. "Determinants of Grain Production and Technological Efficiency in China." *Journal of Agricultural Economics* 49/2 (1998): 171–184.

Zheng, Zheng, Li Ma, Xingping Wang. "China's Real Cropland Area in Qing Dynasty (Qingchao de zhenshi gengdi mianji)." *Jianghai Academic Journal (Jianghai xuekan)* 4 (1998): 129–135.

CHAPTER 5

Understanding China's Agricultural Track Record and Food Security

Abstract This chapter provides a retrospective summary of the key issues in China's agriculture and food security as discussed in this work. In recent years, several countries have reached the upper-middle-income category, possessing purchasing power comparable to that of China. With these latecomers playing an increasingly significant role in the international food market, potential supply and demand imbalances could pose looming food insecurity risks for both China and the global community. Domestically, the issue of rural welfare has diminished as a concern for maintaining farmer's incentives to produce sufficient grain for food self-sufficiency, following the government's shift towards sourcing food supplies from the international commodity market. Despite this, the disparity in income between urban and rural Chinese has persisted. While the Chinese government has announced its aim to achieve "common prosperity," the reality remains starkly different. The aftermath of the post-1979 food economy reforms has been a widened rural-urban income gap, with rural per capita income significantly lower than that in urban areas. Thus, the food sector continues to be a significant yet challenging aspect of the Chinese economy.

Keywords Food (in)security • Dietary transition • Income transition • Semi-vegetarian diet • Animal protein-based diet • International commodity market • Fodder grain • Import dependence • Middle-income countries • Green Revolution

J. Du, *Farmland, Farming and Food in the National Economy of China, 1947–2020*, Palgrave Studies in Economic History, https://doi.org/10.1007/978-3-031-70027-9_5

Key Point Summary

Over time, the Chinese government's strategies for addressing food-related issues have evolved significantly. The food sector is no longer regarded solely as an agricultural or rural concern; it has become increasingly intertwined with industrial growth and urban living. This sector intersects with efforts to reduce poverty, achieve food self-sufficiency and manage inflation-driven consumption prices. Additionally, it impacts domestic politics and international relations through today's interconnected food markets.

- **Terms of Trade and Price Scissors:** Following the Soviet economic model, Mao's approach to rapid industrialisation involved manipulating the intersectoral terms of trade between the food sector and urban industries, especially the heavy industrial sector. In practice, state intervention led to the retention of excessive rural surpluses as a profit margin for industrial development. This was achieved by maintaining two distinct, manipulated pricing systems for agricultural and industrial goods. Theoretically, this practice can be viewed as an intersectoral arbitrage executed by the Maoist government, also known as the "price scissors" used to extract resources and surpluses from the peasantry to fuel industrial expansion.

  The state's intersectoral arbitrage under Mao had two primary objectives. Firstly, it sought to reallocate agricultural surpluses to the industrial sector, providing the necessary capital for fast industrialisation. Secondly, by artificially suppressing food retail prices for urban populations, the government could maintain extremely low urban wages, thereby reducing the financial burden of industrial development. The food sector, further burdened by taxes, bore the full costs of Mao's industrialisation efforts.

  However, this distorted intersectoral terms of trade not only lowered the peasants' incentives to produce but also depressed the returns on their investments in farming. Hence, towards the end of Maoist rural governance, food output had sharply declined, reverting to levels seen in the 1950s. This prolonged agricultural recession was widespread across China under Mao's administration. Before the early 1980s, China's food sector had two main responsibilities: firstly, to fulfil self-sufficiency in staple food grains, and secondly, to facilitate the transfer of agricultural surpluses to support industrialisation, primarily in the urban sector.

- **Food Accessibility and Fiscal Affordability:** Since the reforms began in the 1980s, then central theme of food issues in China has shifted towards alleviating the government's financial burden. This change arose from the unsustainability of the government's monopoly over the food sector in an increasingly market-oriented environment.

The reforming government's approach to food security can be divided into two distinct phases. Before the 2003–2008 reforms, food security was maintained through a state monopoly over the grain production and circulation. This strategy later evolved into a market-based model, complemented by occasional government interventions, such as the use of strategic grain reserves. Specifically, China's food security policies have oscillated between two priorities: maximising production to ensure a steady food supply and maintaining fiscal balance. From 1980 to 2003, the Chinese government's first priority was given to maximising food grain production to safeguard food availability. However, during periods of fiscal strain, often following years of abundant harvest, the emphasis shifted towards achieving fiscal balance, sometimes at the expense of reducing food production. In 2003, significant fiscal challenges compelled the Chinese state to relinquish its monopoly on grain, resulting in a comprehensive period of marketisation and liberalisation that continued through 2003–2008.

It was not until the agricultural reforms of 2003–2008 that China's state-led food security moved beyond the complexities of fiscal pressure and the necessity for rationed food sufficiency. On the one hand, the government was compelled to relinquish control over grain pricing due to fiscal constraints. On the other hand, rising living standards rendered the practice of subsidising urban industry by "squeezing" the food sector[1] unnecessary. However, a distinct trend emerged from food accessibility. Since the mid-2000s, China's CPI has followed a monotonically increasing path, accelerating from 2008 onwards. This upward trend has also affected food retail prices,

[1] For details, refer to Ash, Robert F. "Squeezing the Peasants: Grain Extraction, Food Consumption and Rural Living Standards in Mao's China." *The China Quarterly* 188 (2006): 959–998.

thereby reducing food accessibility for consumers. The surge in food prices attracted increased attention from the central government and sparked considerable interest in rebuilding grain reserves, as outlined in the Medium and Long-term Plan for National Food Security 2008–2020.[2]

- **Dietary Transition and Demand for Fodder Grains:** Economic progress in China's industrial sector has successfully addressed long-standing food security concerns by establishing a balance between food accessibility and affordability. However, increasing wealth among the population has introduced new challenges to maintaining food security. Enhanced income levels have enabled the government to resolve post-war food security issues for staple fodder grains through the consolidation of direct intake supplies. Yet, this success has given rise to a new predicament: the demand for fodder grains now exceeds the country's maximum domestic production capabilities. This change in food security concerns forces the Chinese government to confront critical questions: to what extent is it prepared to rely on the international commodity market for its food supply, and how will it manage the rising food prices associated with such reliance?

There are two ways to address these questions. The first involves leveraging the international food market to narrow the gap between domestic production and consumption. This approach allows China to align domestic consumption with global food prices by trading with countries that have abundant land resources for grain production. The second strategy focuses domestic market price interventions to circumvent import and export restrictions. This method aims to alter the domestic output structure to achieve a supply demand balance across different crop varieties. In practice, China's approach to the international food market has combined elements of both strategies.

The great improvement in income levels has transformed the dietary habits of the Chinese population, transitioning from a primarily vegetarian diet to one richer in animal proteins. Hence,

[2] National Development and Reform Commission of China. ***Medium and Long-term Plan for National Food Security 2008–2020 (Guojia liangshi anquan zhongchangqi guihua gangyao 2008–2020 nian)***. Beijing: National Development and Reform Committee, November 13, 2008.

China's policy on food grain self-sufficiency[3] has been recalibrated: while the demand for rice and wheat is largely met through domestic farming, greater flexibility is afforded to soybeans and maize, which are increasingly imported from the international markets. This change has comprehensively raised China's dependence on food trade, particularly regarding the importation of fodder grains required for animal husbandry.[4]

- **Food Trade and Import Dependence:** China's rapid income growth and the subsequent shift in dietary patterns have led to a strategic increase in the importation of land-intensive agricultural products to meet the growing demand for fodder grains. Since then, China's food security has encountered increasingly complex challenges. The first challenge is addressing hunger and undernourishment, especially in rural areas. The second challenge arises from a shift in dietary preference, moving from a semi-vegetarian diet to one with higher consumption of animal products. This dietary transition has increased the demand for animal fodder, particularly maize and soybeans, impacting the grain sector. As a result, a significant portion of farmland has been reallocated to cultivate these fodder grains, resulting in decreased acreage for staple food grains such as wheat and rice. In response, the Chinese government has prioritised the supply of fodder grains to support changing dietary preferences while reaffirming the "red line" policy for arable land dedicated to major staple food crops. This measure aims to balance accommodating dietary transitions with preserving essential grain supplies, ensuring the maintenance of basic grain rations.

  Since the early 2010s, China has placed a strong emphasis on importing non-staple food crops, especially maize, soybeans and fodder meals (e.g. DDGS). Moreover, the importation of sorghum has gained special importance, underscoring its role in diversifying sources of fodder grains to support the shift towards more animal protein-based diets.

[3] See, Jowett, Alan J. "China's Foodgrains: Production and Performance, 1949–1981." *GeoJournal* 10 (1985): 373–388.

[4] See, Lyons, Thomas P. "Feeding Fujian: Grain Production and Trade, 1986–1996." *The China Quarterly* 155 (1998): 512–545; Du, Jane, and Cheng King. "Unravelling China's Food Security Puzzle, 1979–2008." *The China Quarterly* 235 (2018): 804–827.

Among all countries, China heavily relies on Brazil and the United States for its agricultural product imports. The trade relationship with Brazil is relatively simple, mainly focussing on oilseeds such as soybeans, along with other food-related products like sugar. Different from Brazil, agricultural trade with the United States is more diversified, including soybeans, sorghum and DDGS, with a significant emphasis on the fodder industry. As of 2021, the virtual land use overseas for food imports amounted to 86.4 million hectares, representing 67.7% of China's total farmland availability, which was 127.6 million hectares in 2022. Substituting these agricultural imports with domestic production would necessitate reallocating farmland from food to fodder grain cropping, posing a direct challenge to the Chinese government's goal of achieving staple food grain self-sufficiency. Therefore, continuing to import fodder crops directly is an ideal method to maintain domestic self-sufficiency in staple food grains.

Fodder crops are mainly classified into three categories: energy fodder, protein fodder and prepared fodder. In 2021, China's direct imports of fodder grain were mainly energy fodder, accounting for 77.0%, followed by protein fodder at 22.5%. Excluding domestically produced soybean meals, maize is the primary energy fodder used in poultry farming, while soybean meal serves as the main protein fodder for swine raising. DDGS can partially substitute for both categories. Within the protein fodder category, soybean meals are extensively utilised. Unlike maize, a significant part of soybean meals is derived from domestically processed imported soybeans. This practice of importing large quantities of soybeans has led to substantial soybean meal inventories in China. The presence of large domestic carryover stocks, coupled with tariffs on soybean imports from the United States, is expected to reduce some of the demand for soybean imports.

Agricultural imports reflect the domestic scarcity of per capita land resources in China. By exporting more labour-intensive industrial products while importing cheaper, land-intensive agricultural commodities, China could potentially alter its bargaining power in international economic relations. Since 2018, the impact on China's livestock industry has been significant due to its dependence on fodder-based agricultural imports from the United States. As a major importer of food from the United States, the Chinese government's response to economic tensions between the two countries must consider not only the immediate trade implications but also the broader context of China's overall dependence on food trade and its export of manufactured goods to the United States. The complex interplay underscores the critical and intricate nature of China's decision-making in managing its economic dynamics with the United States.

- **Food Price and Competition in the International Market**: From 2000 to 2020, direct consumption of staple food grains in China decreased from 206 kilogrammes[5] to 135 kilogrammes[6] per person annually. Concurrently, the consumption of meat, aquatic products and dairy increased from 54 kilogrammes to 99 kilogrammes per person per year. This trend was particularly evident among urban households and was further amplified by China's accelerated urbanisation throughout the 2000s and 2010s.

  However, the growing demand for fodder grains in China has far exceeded the reduction in food grain consumption. Since most meat products are produced domestically to meet the needs of the large population, the substantial increase in demand for fodder grain—especially maize and soybeans—has positioned China as the biggest global buyer of these commodities. As a result, China's food security policy has been adjusted: while domestic production of rice and wheat largely satisfies national demand, there is greater flexibility in

[5] "In the year 2000, the food consumption per person in China included 206 kilogrammes of rationed food grains, 110 kilogrammes of vegetables, 8.2 kilogrammes of edible vegetable oil, 7.0 kilogrammes of sugar, 25.3 kilogrammes of meat, 11.8 kilogrammes of eggs, 5.5 kilogrammes of milk, and 11.7 kilogrammes of aquatic products." This data was sourced from the General Office of the State Council of China. "*Document No. 86 of 2001. Circular of the General Office of the State Council on Issuing the Outline of the Programme for Food and Nutrition Development in China (2001–2010) (Guowuyuan bangongting guanyu yinfa zhongguo shiwu yu yingyang fazhan gangyao [2001–2010 nian] de tongzhi).*" Beijing: General Office of the State Council of China, November 3, 2001.

[6] "At the national level, as of 2020, ration food grain consumption in China is expected to be 135 kilogrammes per person per year, with additional consumptions including 12 kilogrammes of edible vegetable oil, 13 kilogrammes of beans, 29 kilogrammes of meat, 16 kilogrammes of eggs, 36 kilogrammes of milk, 18 kilogrammes of aquatic products, 140 kilogrammes of vegetables, and 60 kilogrammes of fruits." For more detailed data, see the General Office of the State Council of China. "*Document No. 3 of 2014. Circular of the General Office of the State Council on Issuing the Outline of the Programme for Food and Nutrition Development in China (2014–2020) (Guowuyuan bangongting guanyu yinfa zhongguo shiwu yu yingyang fazhan gangyao [2014–2020 nian] de tongzhi).*" Beijing: General Office of the State Council of China, January 28, 2014.

sourcing maize and soybeans from the intentional markets. Thus, China's current food security heavily depends on its role and influence in the international food markets, where it competes with other participant countries. Over the past two decades, China's active participation and competitiveness in the international commodity markets have been evident. The growing purchasing power of Chinese consumers has been a significant driving force behind this shift, allowing the Chinese government to offload some of the food supply burdens onto the international market. Nevertheless, China's influence is contested; it faces intense competition from other nations with similar financial capacity, all vying for their share in the international food markets.

China's significant impact on international food markets did not create major turbulence over the past two decades largely because few developing countries underwent a similar dietary transition during this period. As China's purchasing power surged in the 2000s and 2010s, many developing countries were still grappling with slow growth following the economic crises of 1997 and 2008. This situation reduced their competitiveness against China in the international food market. Moreover, China's delayed Green Revolution allowed it to meet its growing food demand through advancements in domestic farming technology. However, with the global economy beginning to recover from the COVID-19 pandemic, the increasing demand from these latecomer countries and their forthcoming competition with China is expected to become a significant concern. This situation, combined with China's substantial domestic food requirement, is likely to impact global food security in the foreseeable future.[7]

- **Ghost Acreage and Food Insecurities**: As industrialisation and urbanisation accelerate in China, the country's food production is increasingly constrained by limited resources and environmental factors. This restriction hampers the ability to enhance food output merely through additional resource inputs. When domestic production fails to meet consumption needs, imports become inevitable.

[7] China's importation of maize has not only driven up maize and poultry prices in certain countries but also signals the potential for significant global repercussions. What was once viewed as a localised issue of China's food security has now evolved into a crucial factor with extensive implications, capable of exerting external shocks across the international food commodity markets.

> Food imports now serve as a vital supplement to domestic resources, allowing for the reallocation of resources to the industrial and service sectors.
>
> Between 2000 and 2022, grain imports facilitated the reallocation of 142.8 million person-years of labour to non-agricultural sectors, accompanied by an investment of $350.6 billion (adjusted to 2015 prices). Had China produced these grains domestically, its non-agricultural GDP growth rate could have been reduced by 17–22% over the past two decades, depending on the TFP method used. This impact would have been even more pronounced—approximately a quarter—if rapeseed and cotton imports had also been considered.

In 2022 alone, China's "ghost acreage"—the farmland required to produce the equivalent of that year's grain imports—totalled 51.8 million hectares. This figure represented approximately 43.5% of China's total grain-sown area for the year, underscoring how the country's rapidly changing dietary patterns have further widened the gap between domestic grain supply and consumption.

Indeed, China has maintained grain output above the international benchmark of 400 kilogrammes per person per year, individual grain consumption has however become increasingly reliant on imports due to the rapidly growing demand for animal protein. According to the National Bureau of Statistics of China, from 2000 to 2022, total consumption of meat (including poultry), poultry eggs and artificially cultured aquatic products increased 2.6-fold, 2.4-fold and 2.1-fold, respectively. Even when accounting for population growth, per capita consumption of meat (including poultry), poultry eggs and artificially cultured aquatic products still rose by 2.3-fold, 2.1-fold and 1.9-fold, respectively. China's rising incomes and urbanisation over the years has further exacerbated the gap between consumption and domestic production. In response to the surging demand for animal-related products, the Chinese government has had to adjust its food security policies,[8] prioritising rice and wheat production

[8] Policy changes focused on the animal industry in the late 2010s are detailed in the General Office of the Ministry of Agriculture and Rural Affairs of China. *Circular of the General Office of Ministry of Agriculture and Rural Affairs on Issuing the Key Points of Works in Livestock Husbandry Industry 2018 (2018 nian xumuye gongzuo yaodian de tongzhi)*. Beijing: General Office of Ministry of Agriculture and Rural Affairs of China, January 30, 2018.

while increasingly relying on international markets to meet a significant portion of its fodder grain needs.

As of 2022, among the four major grain crops—rice, wheat, maize and soybeans—soybean imports have accounted for the largest share of all factor inputs, due to both the high import volume and the monocropping planting technique. For example, net soybean imports in 2022 were approximately 90.5 million tonnes, representing 81.7% of the total soybean consumption that year. Furthermore, around 80% of soybean consumption in China is used for fodder, primarily supporting the animal industries, especially pork production. If we roughly associate pork production with the supply of soybean-derived fodder products, the absence of today's imported soybeans would likely cause individual pork consumption in China to revert to levels seen during the early stages of economic reforms in the 1980s.

While grain imports have alleviated the pressure on China's domestic production inputs, they have also led to an increasingly precarious dependence on imported fodder grain, often referred to as "ghost acreage." Any reduction in land availability directly impacts the country's grain production capacity. Currently, China's cultivated land totals 127.9 million hectares (equivalent to 1.9 billion Chinese mu), just surpassing the 1.8-billion-mu "red line," which represents the minimum threshold needed to meet basic food requirements. However, this is far from sufficient to ensure the diversification of the Chinese diet. As a result, imports of major grain crops are expected to continue rising.

Without the support of food imports to alleviate domestic resource constraints over the past two decades, China's recent non-agricultural GDP growth rate could have been 17–22% slower. With reliance on food imports, imported grain now accounts for half of the domestic grain-sown area and one-third of the total sown area. Given the rising demand for fodder grains due to ongoing dietary transitions, the Chinese government may face increasing food insecurity domestically, despite its efforts to manage them.[9]

[9]There are also concerns that China may face domestic food insecurity in the coming years, starting in 2024, due to the slowing (and at times stagnant) growth of its domestic grain output. For more information, refer to the article by Voice of America. "Why Does Xi Jinping Always Emphasize Food Security? The Lack of Food Security May Be a Major Strategic Weakness for China (Xijinping weisheme zong shi qiangdiao liangshi anquan? Fanwan duan bu lao huo wei zhongguo yi da zhanlue ruanlei)." Published on 26 December 2023. Https://www.voachinese.com/a/7412613.html. Accessed January 15, 2024.

Final Remarks

Mao's ideology in agricultural policy-making led to significant failures in China's agricultural sector. During Mao's era, the majorities of the population during the Mao's era lived at a mere subsistence level, with the peasant class being particularly affected. Low income levels contributed to widespread poverty, and hunger and famine resulted from extremely low food supplies. This was a direct consequence of planned farming policies that caused food production to lag behind population growth. Before the Great Leap Forward in 1957, per person grain output was 301.7 kilogrammes. By 1962, this figure had dropped to 229.5 kilogrammes, a 23.9% decline.

The prolonged recession in China's agriculture left the country unable to meet the basic grain ration needs at 400 kilogrammes per person per year until 1996, when the per capita grain stock finally reached 412.2 kilogrammes. It was at the point that Chinese food availability began to recover from the devastating impacts of Mao's ideology on the farming sector.

Since the CCP's land reforms in the 1940s, the peasant class was transformed into individuals heavily reliant on rural collectives for all productive means and organisational structure. This fundamental change in rural production methods significantly altered individual farmer's production incentives. Meanwhile, during this period, China's entire commercial environment underwent a drastic change, being completely dismantled and replaced with a Soviet-style central planning system. As a result, the social and production organisation of the entire rural sector during the late 1940s and 1950s was restructured to integrate fully into China's closed central planning system. From the perspective of the central planners' ability to extract resources from farming, Mao's transformation of the peasant class and rural farming can be seen as successful. The government assumed complete control over the output and supply of all major staple grains.

To achieve Mao's goal of fast industrialisation, China's agricultural sector, farming practices and the entire peasant class underwent severe disruption and reorganisation. Three key strategies were employed. (1) Mao's authoritarian regime used a centralised planning system to artificially manipulate the relative prices between food and industrial goods. Through systemic arbitrage, a significant portion of rural surplus was diverted to fuel the industrial sector. (2) At the farm gate level, agricultural production collectives monopolised rural labour, land and other forms of capital inputs. These collectives were crucial to Mao's strategy of establishing a state grain monopoly, allowing the government to control all production and sales of agricultural goods. (3) The implementation of the Household Registration System severely restricted interregional and intersectoral labour flows. By controlling labour mobility, the government could allocate labour between sectors according to its developmental priorities, often to the detriment of the farming sector and rural livelihoods.

Mao's stringent control over agricultural inputs and the sale of products began to ease only with the Dengist agricultural reforms in the early 1980s. At the beginning of these economic reforms, the overall Engel's coefficient stood at 63.9% for the year 1978. In the farming sector, this figure was as high as 67.7%.[10]

However, even then, rural labour and capital inputs, including land, remained under strict regulation. Some of Mao's monopolistic practices were not fully abolished until the liberalisation reforms of the entire food sector by the Hu-Wen administration during 2003–2008. Despite all these reforms, the Household Registration System continues to disrupt rural markets to this day. Overall, Mao's mismanagement of the rural economy has had a long-lasting devastating impact on rural livelihoods. In contemporary China, rural households still possess limited decision-making and bargaining power in the markets for agricultural factors and products.

When rural welfare was no longer a concern for maintaining farmers' incentives for food self-sufficiency, following the Chinese government supplementation of the nation's food supply through overseas imports, the income gap between rural and urban areas remained unchanged. Despite the liberalisation of agricultural markets, disparities persisted across the four major categories of residential income: wage income, operational income, capital revenue and transfer payments. Large gaps between rural and urban residents are evident in wage income, capital revenue and transfer payments, while operational income is the only category where rural earnings are comparable to those in the urban sector. The disparity is due to the Household Registration System, which effectively excluded the rural sector from China's superior markets (i.e. labour and capital

[10] For detailed data on Engel's coefficients and living standards in China, please refer to the National Bureau of Statistics of China. National Data. Https://data.stats.gov.cn/english/easyquery.htm. Accessed January 15, 2024.

markets). Rural Chinese have been largely confined to produce and service markets, which remain relatively unregulated. Consequently, these markets have been the primary source of operational income for rural residents.

When the Chinese government announced its goal to achieve "common prosperity,"[11] the reality is however different. The entire rural sector still lacks full access to the capital and labour markets. Moreover, food prices continue to be influenced by grain SOEs. As a result, rural per capita income—whether derived from grain production or non-farming activities—remains significantly lower than urban per capita income. A side effect of the post-1979 economic miracle has been the widening income gap between rural and urban Chinese. China's food sector remains as the elephant in the room of the contemporary Chinese economy.

References

Ash, Robert F. "Squeezing the Peasants: Grain Extraction, Food Consumption and Rural Living Standards in Mao's China." *The China Quarterly* 188 (2006): 959–998.

Deng Xiaoping. *Selected Works of Deng Xiaoping* Volume III. Beijing: People's Publishing House (Renmin chuban she), 1993.

General Office of the Ministry of Agriculture and Rural Affairs of China. "*Circular of the General Office of Ministry of Agriculture and Rural Affairs on Issuing the Key Points of Works in Livestock Husbandry Industry 2018 (2018 nian xumuye gongzuo yaodian de tongzhi).*" Beijing: General Office of Ministry of Agriculture and Rural Affairs of China, January 30, 2018.

General Office of the State Council of China. "*Document No. 3 of 2014. Circular of the General Office of the State Council on Issuing the Outline of the Programme for Food and Nutrition Development in China (2014–2020) (Guowuyuan bangongting guanyu yinfa zhongguo shiwu yu yingyang fazhan gangyao [2014–2020 nian] de tongzhi).*" Beijing: General Office of the State Council of China, January 28, 2014.

General Office of the State Council of China. "*Document No. 86 of 2001. Circular of the General Office of the State Council on Issuing the Outline of the Programme for Food and Nutrition Development in China (2001–2010) (Guowuyuan bangongting guanyu yinfa zhongguo shiwu yu yingyang fazhan gangyao [2001–2010 nian] de tongzhi).*" Beijing: General Office of the State Council of China, November 3, 2001.

[11] Deng Xiaoping. *Selected Works of Deng Xiaoping* Volume III. Beijing: People's Publishing House (Renmin chuban she), 1993.

Jowett, Alan J. "China's Foodgrains: Production and Performance, 1949–1981." *GeoJournal* 10 (1985): 373–388.

National Bureau of Statistics of China. National Data. Https://data.stats.gov.cn/english/easyquery.htm. Accessed January 15, 2024.

National Development and Reform Commission of China. *Medium and Long-term Plan for National Food Security 2008–2020 (Guojia liangshi anquan zhongchangqi guihua gangyao 2008–2020 nian)*. Beijing: National Development and Reform Committee, 13 November 2008.

Voice of America. "Why Does Xi Jinping Always Emphasize Food Security? The Lack of Food Security May Be a Major Strategic Weakness for China (Xijinping weisheme zong shi qiangdiao liangshi anquan? Fanwan duan bu lao huo wei zhongguo yi da zhanlue ruanlei)." Published on 26 December 2023. Https://www.voachinese.com/a/7412613.html. Accessed January 15, 2024.

Index[1]

[1] Note: Page numbers followed by 'n' refer to notes.

J. Du, *Farmland, Farming and Food in the National Economy of China, 1947–2020*, Palgrave Studies in Economic History,
https://doi.org/10.1007/978-3-031-70027-9

M

N

O

P

R

S

The manufacturer's authorised representative in the EU is Springer Nature Customer Service Centre GmbH, Europaplatz 3, 69115 Heidelberg, Germany. If you have any concerns regarding our products, please contact ProductSafety@springernature.com

Printed and bound by CPI Group (UK) Ltd, Croydon, CR0 4YY
30/09/2026
02225472-0007